Problems on Algorithms

Ian Parberry

Department of Computer Sciences
University of North Texas

Prentice Hall, Englewood Cliffs, New Jersey 07632

Library of Congress Cataloging-in-Publication Data

Parberry, Ian.
    Problems on algorithms / Ian Parberry.
        p.   cm.
    Includes bibliographical references and index.
    ISBN 0-13-433558-9
    1. Computer algorithms.   I. Title.
QA76.9.A43P37 1995
005.1--dc20
                                                                94-48519
                                                                CIP

Acquisitions Editor: Marcia Horton
Production Editor: Joe Scordato
Copy Editor: Peter Zurita
Cover Designer: Maureen Eide
Buyer: Lori Bulwin
Editorial Assistant : Dolores Mars

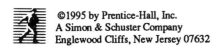 ©1995 by Prentice-Hall, Inc.
A Simon & Schuster Company
Englewood Cliffs, New Jersey 07632

The author and publisher of this book have used their best efforts in preparing this book. These efforts
include the development, research, and testing of the theories and programs to determine their effectiveness.
The author and publisher make no warranty of any kind, expressed or implied, with regard to these programs
or the documentation contained in this book. The author and publisher shall not be liable in any event for
incidental or consequential damages in connection with, or arising out of, the furnishing, performance, or use
of these programs.

Printed in the United States of America

10 9 8 7 6 5 4 3 2 1

005.1
P224p
1995

0-13-433558-9

Prentice-Hall International (UK) Limited, London
Prentice-Hall of Australia Pty. Limited, Sydney
Prentice-Hall Canada Inc., Toronto
Prentice-Hall Hispanoamericana, S.A., Mexico
Prentice-Hall of India Private Limited, New Delhi
Prentice-Hall of Japan, Inc., Tokyo
Simon & Schuster Asia Pte. Ltd., Singapore
Editora Prentice-Hall do Brasil, Ltda., Rio de Janeiro

Contents

Preface

The ability to devise effective and efficient algorithms in new situations is a skill that separates the master programmer from the merely adequate coder. The best way to develop that skill is to solve problems. To be effective problem solvers, master-programmers-in-training must do more than memorize a collection of standard techniques and applications — they must in addition be able to internalize and integrate what they have learned and apply it in new circumstances. This book is a collection of problems on the design, analysis, and verification of algorithms for use by practicing programmers who wish to hone and expand their skills, as a supplementary text for students enrolled in an undergraduate or beginning graduate class on algorithms, and as a self-study text for graduate students who are preparing for the qualifying (often called "breadth" or "comprehensive") examination on algorithms for a Ph.D. program in Computer Science or Computer Engineering. It is intended to augment the problem sets found in any standard algorithms textbook.

Recognizing that a supplementary text must be cost-effective if it is to be useful, I have made two important and perhaps controversial decisions in order to keep its length within reasonable bounds. The first is to cover only what I consider to be the most important areas of algorithm design and analysis. Although most instructors throw in a "fun" advanced topic such as amortized analysis, computational geometry, approximation algorithms, number-theoretic algorithms, randomized algorithms, or parallel algorithms, I have chosen not to cover these areas. The second decision is not to search for the origin of the problems that I have used. A lengthy discussion of the provenance of each problem would help make this book more scholarly, but would not make it more attractive for its intended audience — students and practicing programmers.

To make this book suitable for self-instruction, I have provided at the end of each chapter a small collection of hints, solutions, and comments. The solutions are necessarily few for reasons of brevity, and also to avoid hindering instructors in their selection of homework problems. I have included various preambles that summarize the background knowledge needed to solve the problems so that students who are familiar with the notation and style of their textbook and instructor can become more familiar with mine.

The organization of this book is a little unusual and requires a few words of explanation. After a chapter of introduction, it begins with five chapters on background material that most algorithms instructors would like their students to have mastered before setting foot in an algorithms class. This will be the case at some universities, but even then most students would profit from brushing up on this material by attempting a few of the problems. The introductory chapters include mathematical induction, big-O notation, recurrence relations, correctness proofs, and basic algorithm analysis methods. The correctness proof chapter goes beyond what is normally taught, but I believe that students profit from it once they overcome their initial aversion to mathematical formalism.

The next four chapters are organized by algorithm design technique: divide-and-conquer, dynamic programming, greedy algorithms, and exhaustive search. This organization is somewhat nonstandard, but I believe that the pedagogical benefits outweigh the drawbacks (the most significant of which seems to be the scattering of problems on graph algorithms over several chapters, mainly in Sections 2.10, 2.11, 7.7, 8.4, 9.2, 9.3, 9.4, 13.3, and 13.4). Standard textbooks usually devote little time to exhaustive search because it usually requires exponential time, which is a pity when it contains many rich and interesting opportunities to practice the application of algorithm design, analysis, and verification methods. The manuscript is rounded out with chapters on advanced data structures and $\mathcal{NP}$-completeness. The final chapter contains miscellaneous problems that do not necessarily fit into the earlier chapters, and those for which part of the problem is to determine the algorithmic technique or techniques to be used.

The algorithms in this book are expressed in a Pascal-like pseudocode. Two problems (Problems 326 and 327) require the reader to examine some code written in Pascal, but the details of the programming language are not a major factor in the solutions. In any case, I believe that students of Computer Science should be literate in many different programming languages.

For those who are interested in technical details, this manuscript was produced from camera-ready copy provided by the author using LATEX version 2.09 (which used TEX C Version 3.14t3), using the Prentice Hall macros `phstyle.sty` written by J. Kenneth Shultis, and the `twoside`, `epsf`, and `makeidx` style files. The Bibliography was created by BibTEX. The index was produced using the program `makeindex`. The figures were prepared in encapsulated Postscript form using `idraw`, and the graphs using `xgraph`. The `dvi` file produced by LATEX was translated into Postscript using `dvips`.

A list of errata for this book is available by anonymous `ftp` from `ftp.unt.edu` (IP address 129.120.1.1), in the directory `ian/poa`. I will be grateful to receive feedback, suggestions, errata, and in particular any new and interesting problems (including those from areas not presently covered), which can be sent by electronic mail to `ian@ponder.csci.unt.edu`.

Chapter 1

Introduction

Problems on Algorithms contains 668 problems on the design, verification, and analysis of algorithms. This chapter is the only background that you will get before we start listing problems. It is divided into four sections. The first section describes the philosophy of this book and how to get the best out of it. The second section contains an overview of the remaining chapters. The third section briefly touches on the pseudocode used to describe algorithms. The fourth section gives a quick review of some of the textbooks available on algorithms and related subjects.

1.1 HOW TO USE THIS BOOK

Most chapters have sections with hints for, solutions to, and comments on selected problems. It is recommended that readers first attempt the problems on their own. The hints should be consulted only when encountering serious difficulty in getting started. The solutions can be used as examples of the type of answers that are expected. Only a limited number of solutions are given so that students are not tempted to peek, and to ensure that there remains a large number of problems that instructors can assign as homework.

Each problem is labeled with a sequence of icons. The more mortarboards 🎓 a problem has, the more difficult it is. Problems with one or two mortarboards are suitable for a senior-level undergraduate class on algorithms. Problems with two or three mortarboards are suitable for a graduate class on algorithms. The remaining icons indicate the existence of additional material: The lightbulb 💡 indicates that there is a hint, the scroll and feather 🖋 indicates that there is a solution, and the smiley face 😊 indicates that there is a comment. This is summarized for the reader's convenience in Table 1.1.

1.2 OVERVIEW OF CHAPTERS

Chapters 2–4 contain problems on some background material on discrete mathematics that students should already have met before entering an undergraduate algorithms course; respectively mathematical induction, big-O notation, and recurrence relations. If you are a student in an algorithms class, I strongly recommend

Symbol	Meaning
🎓	easy
🎓 🎓	medium
🎓 🎓 🎓	difficult
💡	hint
📖	solution
😊💬	comment

Table 1.1. Problem symbols and their meaning.

that you review this material and attempt some of the problems from Chapters 2–4 before attending the first class. Some kind instructors may spend a few lectures "reminding" you of this material, but not all of them can afford the time to do so. In any case, you will be ahead of the game if you devote some time to look over the material again. If you ignored the material on mathematical induction in your discrete mathematics class, thinking that it is useless to a programmer, then think again. If you can master induction, you have mastered recursion — they are two sides of the same coin.

You may also meet the material from Chapters 5 and 6 in other classes. Chapter 5 contains problems on correctness proofs. Not all instructors will emphasize correctness proofs in their algorithms class, but mastering them will teach you important skills in formalization, expression, and design. The approach to correctness proofs taken in Chapter 5 is closer to that taken by working researchers than the formal-logic approach expounded by others such as Dijkstra [21]. Chapter 6 contains some problems involving the analysis of some naive algorithms. You should have met this material in earlier classes, but you probably don't have the depth of knowledge and facility that you can get from working the problems in this chapter.

Chapters 7–10 consist of problems on various algorithm design techniques: respectively, divide-and-conquer, dynamic programming, greedy algorithms, and exhaustive search. The problems address some of the standard applications of these techniques, and ask you to demonstrate your knowledge by applying the techniques to new problems. Divide-and-conquer has already been foreshadowed in earlier chapters, but the problems in Chapter 7 will test your knowledge further. The treatment of exhaustive search in Chapter 10 goes beyond what is normally covered in algorithms courses. The excuse for skimming over exhaustive search is usually a natural distate for exponential time algorithms. However, extensive problems are provided here because exhaustive search contains many rich and interesting opportunities to practice the application of algorithm design, analysis, and verification methods.

Chapter 11 contains problems on advanced data structures, and Chapter 12 contains problems on $\mathcal{NP}$-completeness, Finally, Chapter 13 contains miscellaneous problems, defined to be those that do not necessarily fit into the earlier chapters, and those for which part of the problem is to determine the algorithmic technique to be used.

1.3   PSEUDOCODE

The algorithms in this text are described in a Pascal-like pseudocode. Here is a quick overview of the conventions used:

Data Types: Most variables are either integers or one- or two-dimensional arrays of integers. The notation $P[i..j]$ is shorthand for an array P, whose elements are $P[i], P[i+1], \ldots, P[j]$. Occasionally, variables will be other mathematical objects such as sets or lists.

Block-Structuring: Indentation is used to indicate block-structuring, in an attempt to save space.

Assignment Statements: The ":=" symbol is the assignment operator.

Sequencing: A sequence of commands will be on separate lines or separated by semicolons.

Selection: The selection command uses Pascal's **if-then-else** syntax, which has the form

$$\text{if condition}$$
$$\textbf{then } S_1$$
$$\textbf{else } S_2$$

If the condition is `true` at time of execution, then S_1 is executed; otherwise S_2 is executed. The **else** clause will be omitted if it is empty.

Indefinite Iteration: Indefinite iteration uses Pascal's pre-tested **while** loop or post-tested **repeat** loop. The **while** loop has the form

$$\textbf{while condition do}$$
$$S$$

If the condition is `true`, then S is executed. The condition is then re-evaluated. If it is `false`, the loop terminates. Otherwise S is executed again. The process repeats until the condition is `false`. The **repeat** loop has the form

$$\textbf{repeat}$$
$$S$$
$$\textbf{until condition}$$

and is equivalent to

$$
S \\
\textbf{while } \text{not condition } \textbf{do} \\
S
$$

Definite Iteration: Definite (count-controlled) iteration is achieved using Pascal's
for loop. Some loops count up (using the keyword **to**), and some count
down (using the keyword **downto**). An upward-counting for-loop will be
done zero times if the start value is larger than the finish value (analogously
for downward-counting for-loops). The syntax is as follows, with the upward-
counting loop on the left, and the downward-counting loop on the right:

$$
\begin{array}{ll}
\textbf{for } i := s \textbf{ to } f \textbf{ do} & \qquad \textbf{for } i := s \textbf{ downto } f \textbf{ do} \\
\quad S & \qquad \quad S
\end{array}
$$

which are equivalent to, respectively,

$$
\begin{array}{ll}
i := s & \qquad i := s \\
\textbf{while } i \leq f \textbf{ do} & \qquad \textbf{while } i \geq f \textbf{ do} \\
\quad S & \qquad \quad S \\
\quad i := i + 1 & \qquad \quad i := i - 1
\end{array}
$$

Subroutines and Parameters: Subroutines are expressed using Pascal-style **procedure**s and **function**s. Functions return a value, which unlike Pascal may
be a complicated object. I have chosen to follow the lead of Aho, Hopcroft,
and Ullman [2] in using a C-like **return** statement to describe the value returned by a function. Procedures return values through their parameters.
Most parameters are value parameters, though some are variable parameters.
You'll be able to tell the difference by context — those that return values are
obviously variable parameters! Comments in the algorithms should give you
an extra hint.

1.4 USEFUL TEXTS

There are many good algorithms texts available, and more get published every
year. Here is a quick thumbnail sketch of some of them, and some related texts
that you might find useful. I recommend that the conscientious student examine
as many texts as possible in the library and choose one that suits their individual
taste. Remember, though, that different texts have differing areas of strength, and
appeal to different types of reader. I also strongly recommend that the practicing
programmer include in their library a copy of Bentley [9, 10]; Cormen, Leiserson,
and Rivest [19]; Garey and Johnson [28]; Graham, Knuth, and Patashnik [30]; and
Knuth [45, 46, 47].

Aho, Hopcroft, and Ullman [1] This was the standard graduate text on algorithms and data structures for many years. It is written quite tersely, with some sentences requiring a paragraph of explanation for some students. If you want the plain facts with no singing or dancing, this is the book for you. It is a little dated in presentation and material, but not particularly so.

Aho, Hopcroft, and Ullman [2] This is the undergraduate version of the previous book, with more emphasis on programming. It is full of minor errors. A large number of the Pascal program fragments don't work, even when you correctly implement their C-like **return** statement.

Aho and Ullman [3] This textbook is redefining the undergraduate computer science curriculum at many leading institutions. It is a good place to go to brush up on your discrete mathematics, data structures, and problem solving skills.

Baase [7] A good algorithms text at the upper-division undergraduate level.

Bentley [9, 10] This delightful pair of books are a collection of Jon Bentley's Programming Pearls column from *Communications of the ACM*. They should be recommended reading for all undergraduate computer science majors. Bentley explores the problems and pitfalls of algorithm design and analysis, and pays careful attention to implementation and experimentation. The subjects chosen are too idiosyncratic and anecdotal to be a textbook, but nonetheless a useful pair of books.

Brassard and Bratley [14] This is another good algorithms text with a strong emphasis on design techniques. The title comes from the French word *algorithmique*, which is what they (perhaps more aptly) call Computer Science.

Cormen, Leiserson, and Rivest [19] This is an excellent text for those who can handle it. In the spirit of Aho, Hopcroft, and Ullman [1], it does not mess around. A massive tome, it contains enough material for both a graduate and undergraduate course in algorithms. It is the definitive text for those who want to get right down to business, but it is not for the faint of heart.

Even [26] This is the canonical book on graph algorithms covering most of the graph algorithm material taught in the typical algorithms course, plus more. It is a little dated, but still very useful.

Garey and Johnson [28] This is the canonical book on $\mathcal{NP}$-completeness. It is particularly useful for its large list of $\mathcal{NP}$-complete problems. It is showing its age a little, but David Johnson has expressed an intention to work on a Second Edition. More modern subjects are covered by David Johnson in "The NP-Completeness Column: An On-Going Guide" published on a semiregular basis in *Journal of Algorithms* (the latest was in September 1992, but David Johnson recently assured me that more are planned).

Gibbons [29] A more modern and carefully presented text on graph algorithms, superior in many ways to Even [26].

Graham, Knuth, and Patashnik [30] An excellent book on discrete mathematics for computer science. However, many students find it quite difficult going. It is noted for its marginal (and often obscure) graffiti.

Greene and Knuth [33] A highly mathematical text for an advanced course on algorithm analysis at Stanford. Recommended for the serious graduate student.

Harel [34] This is another good text along the lines of Brassard and Bratley. It contains excellent high-level descriptions of subjects that tend to confuse the beginning student if they are presented in all their detailed glory. It is noted for its biblical quotes.

Horowitz and Sahni [37] This is a reasonable text for many of the topics found in the typical algorithms class, but it is weak on analysis and but its approach to backtracking is somewhat idiosyncratic and hard to follow.

Kingston [44] A strong textbook for the elementary undergraduate algorithms course, but the coverage is a little shallow for advanced undergraduates. The chapter on correctness proofs is an unusual but welcome addition. Divide-and-conquer and dynamic programming are covered very sketchily, and the approach to greedy algorithms is idiosyncratic but likely to strike a chord with some students.

Knuth [45, 46, 47] The Knuth three-volume series is the standard reference text for researchers and students. The material in it has aged well, except for Knuth's penchant for an obscure fictitious assembly-level code instead of the more popular and easy to understand pseudocode.

Kozen [50] A text for graduate students containing 40 lectures on algorithms. The terse presentation is not for everybody. It contains enough material for a single graduate course, as opposed to the normal text that allows the instructor to pick and choose the material to be covered. The choice of material is strong but not to everybody's taste. The homework problems (all of which have solutions) and miscellaneous exercises (some of which have solutions) are particularly useful.

Lewis and Denenberg [52] A strong data structures text that also covers some of the material in the typical algorithms course.

Manber [56] Some students find the approach taken in this book, which is algorithm design by successive refinement of intuitive but flawed version of the algorithm, very helpful. Others, who do not think this way, hate it. It is certainly more realistic in its approach to algorithm design than more formal texts, but perhaps it encourages the wrong habits. Some important topics are not covered in very great detail.

Moret and Shapiro [58] This is planned as the first volume of a two-volume set. This volume covers tractable problems, and the second volume (unsighted as yet) will cover intractable problems. It has a definite combinatorial optimization flavor. Dynamic programming is a notable omission from the first volume.

Papadimitriou and Steiglitz [59] A reasonable text for an algorithms course, but one which is very heavy with the jargon and mind-set of the combinatorial optimization and numerical analysis community, which makes it a difficult book to just dip into at random for the parts of it that are useful.

Purdom and Brown [64] A mathematically rigorous text that focuses on analysis almost to the exclusion of design principles.

Rawlins [67] An entertaining text that nonetheless is technically rigorous and detailed.

Sedgewick [72] This book studies a large array of standard algorithms, but it is largely descriptive in nature and does not spend much time on verification, analysis, or design techniques. It is excellent for the elementary undergraduate algorithms curriculum, but not sufficiently rigorous for upper-division courses.

Smith [74] This is another strong algorithms text with an awesome collection of problems.

Solow [75] This is a good text for the student who has trouble with mathematical formalism. The chapter on induction may be particularly useful for those who have trouble getting started.

Weiss [82] A strong data structures text that also covers quite a bit of the material in the typical algorithms course.

Wilf [83] A book that does a good job on analysis, but does not cover algorithm design techniques. The selection of topics is limited to chapters on mathematical preliminaries, recursion, network flow, number-theoretic algorithms, and $\mathcal{NP}$-completeness.

Chapter 2

Mathematical Induction

At first sight, this chapter may seem out of place because it doesn't seem to be about algorithms at all. Although the problems in this chapter are mainly mathematical in nature and have very little to do with algorithms, they are good practice in a technique that is fundamental to algorithm design, verification, and analysis. Unfortunately, many students come to my algorithms class poorly versed in the use of induction. Either it was badly taught or they discarded it as useless information (or both). If you are one of these students, you should start by attempting at least some of the following problems. In addition to mastering the *technique* of mathematical induction, you should pay particular attention to the results in Sections 2.1, 2.2, 2.3, 2.7, 2.8, 2.10, and 2.11. Some of them are quite useful in algorithm design and analysis, as we shall see later.

2.1 SUMMATIONS

1. 🎓📝😊 Prove by induction on $n \geq 0$ that $\sum_{i=1}^{n} i = n(n+1)/2$.

2. 🎓 Prove by induction on $n \geq 0$ that $\sum_{i=1}^{n} i^2 = n(n+1)(2n+1)/6$.

3. 🎓😊 Prove by induction on $n \geq 0$ that $\sum_{i=1}^{n} i^3 = n^2(n+1)^2/4$.

4. 🎓😊 Prove by induction on $n \geq 0$ that

$$\sum_{i=0}^{n}(2i+1)^2 = (n+1)(2n+1)(2n+3)/3.$$

5. 🎓😊 Prove by induction on $n \geq 0$ that $\sum_{i=1}^{n} i(i+1) = n(n+1)(n+2)/3$.

6. 🎓😊 Prove by induction on $n \geq 0$ that

$$\sum_{i=1}^{n} i(i+1)(i+2) = n(n+1)(n+2)(n+3)/4.$$

8

7. ☞ Prove by induction on $n \geq 0$ that $\sum_{i=1}^{n} i \cdot i! = (n+1)! - 1$.

8. ☞ ✑ Prove by induction on $n \geq 1$ that $\sum_{i=1}^{n} 1/2^i = 1 - 1/2^n$.

9. ☞ ☺✐ Prove by induction on $n \geq 1$ that for every $a \neq 1$,

$$\sum_{i=0}^{n} a^i = \frac{a^{n+1} - 1}{a - 1}.$$

10. ☞ ☺✐ Prove by induction on $n \geq 0$ that for every $a \neq 1$, and all $0 \leq j \leq n$,

$$\sum_{i=j}^{n} a^i = \frac{a^{n+1} - a^j}{a - 1}.$$

11. ☞ ✑ ☺✐ Prove by induction on $n \geq 0$ that $\sum_{i=0}^{n} 2^i = 2^{n+1} - 1$.

12. ☞ Prove by induction on $n \geq 1$ that

$$\sum_{i=1}^{n} \frac{1}{i(i+1)} = \frac{n}{n+1}.$$

13. ☞ ☺✐ Prove by induction on $n \geq 0$ that $\sum_{i=1}^{n} i2^i = (n-1)2^{n+1} + 2$.

14. ☞ Prove by induction on $n \geq 0$ that for every $a \neq 1$,

$$\sum_{i=1}^{n} ia^i = \frac{na^{n+2} - (n+1)a^{n+1} + a}{(a-1)^2}.$$

15. ☞ ☺✐ Prove by induction on $n \geq 0$ that

$$\sum_{i=1}^{n} i^2 2^i = n^2 2^{n+1} - n2^{n+2} + 3 \cdot 2^{n+1} - 6.$$

16. ☞ ☺✐ Prove by induction on $n \geq 0$ that

$$\sum_{i=1}^{n} i^2 2^{n-i} = 2^{n+3} - 2^{n+1} - n^2 - 4n - 6.$$

17. ☞ Prove by induction on $n \geq 0$ that

$$\sum_{i=1}^{n} \frac{1}{n+i} = \sum_{i=1}^{n} \left(\frac{1}{2i-1} - \frac{1}{2i} \right).$$

2.2 INEQUALITIES

18. Prove by induction on $n \geq 1$ that if $x > -1$, then $(1+x)^n \geq 1 + nx$.

19. Prove by induction on $n \geq 7$ that $3^n < n!$.

20. Prove by induction on $n \geq 5$ that $2^n > n^2$.

21. Prove by induction on $k \geq 1$ that $\sum_{i=1}^{n} i^k \leq n^k(n+1)/2$.

22. Prove by induction on $n \geq 0$ that

$$\sum_{i=1}^{n} \frac{1}{i^2} < 2 - \frac{1}{n}.$$

23. Prove by induction that if $n \geq 4$ is even, and $2 \leq i \leq n/2$, then

$$\sum_{k=1}^{i} \prod_{j=1}^{k} (n - 2j + 1) \leq 2 \prod_{j=1}^{i} (n - 2j + 1).$$

2.3 FLOORS AND CEILINGS

Suppose $x \in \mathbf{R}^+$. The *floor* of x, denoted $\lfloor x \rfloor$, is defined to be the largest integer that is no larger than x. The *ceiling* of x, denoted $\lceil x \rceil$, is defined to be the smallest integer that is no smaller than x.

24. Prove by induction on $n \geq 0$ that

$$\left\lfloor \frac{n}{2} \right\rfloor = \begin{cases} n/2 & \text{if } n \text{ is even} \\ (n-1)/2 & \text{if } n \text{ is odd.} \end{cases}$$

25. Prove by induction on $n \geq 0$ that

$$\left\lceil \frac{n}{2} \right\rceil = \begin{cases} n/2 & \text{if } n \text{ is even} \\ (n+1)/2 & \text{if } n \text{ is odd.} \end{cases}$$

26. Prove by induction on $n \geq 1$ that for all $m \in \mathbf{R}^+$,

$$\left\lceil \frac{n}{m} \right\rceil = \left\lfloor \frac{n+m-1}{m} \right\rfloor.$$

2.4 DIVISIBILITY

27. ☞ ⌨ Prove by induction on $n \geq 0$ that $n^3 + 2n$ is divisible by 3.

28. ☞ Prove by induction on $n \geq 0$ that $n^5 - n$ is divisible by 5.

29. ☞ Prove by induction on $n \geq 0$ that $5^{n+1} + 2 \cdot 3^n + 1$ is divisible by 8.

30. ☞ Prove by induction on $n \geq 0$ that $8^{n+2} + 9^{2n+1}$ is divisible by 73.

31. ☞ Prove by induction that for all $n \geq 0$, $11^{n+2} + 12^{2n+1}$ is divisible by 133.

32. ☞☞ Define $S \subseteq \mathbb{N} \times \mathbb{N}$ as follows. $(0,0) \in S$. If $(m,n) \in S$, then $(m+2, n+3) \in S$. Prove by induction on $n \geq 0$ that for all $(m,n) \in S$, $m+n$ is divisible by 5.

33. ☞ Prove by induction that a decimal number is divisible by 3 iff the sum of its digits is divisible by 3.

34. ☞ Prove by induction that a decimal number is divisible by 9 iff the sum of its digits is divisible by 9.

35. ☞ Prove by induction that the sum of the cubes of three successive natural numbers is divisible by 9.

36. ☞☞ Let $S_n = \{1, 2, \ldots, 2n\}$ be the set of integers from 1 to $2n$. Let $T \subset S_n$ be any subset containing exactly $n+1$ elements of S_n. Prove by induction on n that there exists $x, y \in T$, $x \neq y$, such that x divides evenly into y with no remainder.

2.5 POSTAGE STAMPS

37. ☞ 💡 ⌨ Show that any integer postage greater than 7 cents can be formed by using only 3-cent and 5-cent stamps.

38. ☞ Show that any integer postage greater than 34 cents can be formed by using only 5-cent and 9-cent stamps.

39. ☞ Show that any integer postage greater than 5 cents can be formed by using only 2-cent and 7-cent stamps.

40. ☞ Show that any integer postage greater than 59 cents can be formed by using only 7-cent and 11-cent stamps.

41. ☞☞ What is the smallest value of k such that any integer postage greater than k cents can be formed by using only 4-cent and 9-cent stamps? Prove your answer correct.

42. ☜☜ What is the smallest value of k such that any integer postage greater than k cents can be formed by using only 6-cent and 11-cent stamps? Prove your answer correct.

43. ☜☜ Show that for all $n \geq 1$, any positive integer amount of postage that is at least $n(n-1)$ cents can be formed by using only n-cent and $(n+1)$-cent stamps.

44. ☜☜ Show that for all $m, n \geq 1$ such that $\gcd(m,n) = 1$, there exists $k \in \mathbf{N}$ such that any positive integer amount of postage that is at least k cents can be formed by using only m-cent and n-cent stamps.

2.6 CHESSBOARD PROBLEMS

45. ☜ Prove by induction that for all $n \in \mathbf{N}$ and all even $m \in \mathbf{N}$, an $n \times m$ chessboard has exactly the same number of black squares and white squares.

46. ☜ Prove by induction that for all odd $n, m \in \mathbf{N}$, an $n \times m$ chessboard has all four corner squares colored the same.

47. ☜ ☺☞ Prove by induction that for all odd $n, m \in \mathbf{N}$, an $n \times m$ chessboard with the corner squares colored white has one more white square than black square.

48. ☜☜ ☀ ☺☞ Recall that a knight can make one of eight legal moves depicted in Figure 2.1. Figure 2.2 shows a *closed knight's tour* on an 8×8 chessboard, that is, a circular tour of knight's moves that visits every square of the chessboard exactly once before returning to the first square. Prove by induction that a closed knight's tour exists for any $2^k \times 2^k$ chessboard for all $k \geq 3$.

A *triomino* is an "L"-shaped tile formed by three adjacent squares of a chessboard, shown in Figure 2.3. An arrangement of triominoes is a *tiling* of a chessboard if it covers it exactly without overlap, except for one square which is missed. For example, Figure 2.4 shows a chessboard with a missing square filled in black on the left, and a tiling with triominos that covers every square of the board except this one on the right.

49. ☜☜ ☀ Prove by induction on $n \geq 1$ that any $2^n \times 2^n$ chessboard that is missing one square can be tiled with triominoes, regardless of where the missing square is.

50. ☜☜ Prove or disprove that all chessboards of the following dimensions can be tiled by triominoes: (a) 3×2^n, (b) 6×2^n, (c) $3^n \times 3^n$, (d) $6^n \times 6^n$.

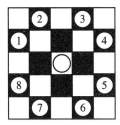

Figure 2.1. The eight legal moves that a knight on the center square can make.

Figure 2.2. A closed knight's tour on an 8 × 8 chessboard.

Figure 2.3. A triomino.

Figure 2.4. A chessboard with a missing square filled in black (left), and a tiling with triominos that covers every square of the board except the missing one (right).

51. 🎓🎓🎓 ☺ Prove that any $2^n \times 2^n$ chessboards with one square missing can be tiled by triominoes of only three colors so that no pair of triominoes that share an edge have the same color.

2.7 FIBONACCI NUMBERS

The Fibonacci numbers F_n for $(n \geq 0)$ are defined recursively as follows: $F_0 = 0$, $F_1 = 1$, and for $n \geq 2$, $F_n = F_{n-1} + F_{n-2}$.

52. 🎓 📜 Prove by induction on n that $\sum_{i=0}^{n} F_i = F_{n+2} - 1$.

53. 🎓 💡 Prove by induction that $F_{n+k} = F_k F_{n+1} + F_{k-1} F_n$.

54. 🎓 Prove by induction on $n \geq 1$ that $\sum_{i=1}^{n} F_i^2 = F_n F_{n+1}$.

55. 🎓 Prove by induction on $n \geq 1$ that $F_{n+1} F_{n+2} = F_n F_{n+3} + (-1)^n$.

56. 🎓 Prove by induction on $n \geq 2$ that $F_{n-1} F_{n+1} = F_n^2 + (-1)^n$.

2.8 BINOMIAL COEFFICIENTS

The binomial coefficient

$$\binom{n}{r},$$

for $n, r \in \mathbb{N}$, $r \leq n$, is defined to be the number of ways of choosing r things from n without replacement, that is,

$$\binom{n}{r} = \frac{n!}{r!(n-r)!}.$$

57. 🎓 💡 Prove by induction on n that

$$\sum_{m=0}^{n} \binom{n}{m} = 2^n.$$

58. 🎓 Prove by induction on $n \geq 1$ that for all $1 \leq m \leq n$,

$$\binom{n}{m} \leq n^m.$$

59. 🎓 Prove by induction on n that

$$(a+b)^n = \sum_{m=0}^{n} \binom{n}{m} a^m b^{n-m}.$$

60. 🎓 ☺ Prove by induction on n that for all even n, if $k \neq n/2$, then

$$\binom{n}{n/2} > \binom{n}{k}.$$

61. 🎓 ☺ Prove by induction on n that for all even n,

$$\binom{n}{n/2} = \Omega(2^n/n).$$

62. 🎓 ☺ Prove by induction that for all $n \in \mathbb{N}$,

$$\sum_{i=0}^{n} i \cdot \binom{n}{i} = n2^{n-1}.$$

63. 🎓 Prove by induction that for all $n \in \mathbb{N}$,

$$\sum_{i=0}^{n} 2^{-i} \cdot \binom{n}{i} = (3/2)^n.$$

2.9   WHAT IS WRONG?

64. 🎓 ☺ What, if anything is wrong with the following reasoning? All horses are the same color. The proof is by induction on the number of horses. The base of the induction is easy: If there is one horse, then it is trivially the same color as itself. Now suppose that there are n horses, numbered 1 through n. By the induction hypothesis, horses 1 through $n-1$ have the same color (let's say black). In particular, horse 2 is black. Also by the induction hypothesis, horses 2 through n have the same color. Since horse 2 is black, this means that horses 2 through n must be black. Therefore, all of the horses have the same color.

65. 🎓 What is wrong with the following proof? We claim that $6n = 0$ for all $n \in \mathbb{N}$. The proof is by induction on $n \geq 0$. Clearly, if $n = 0$, then $6n = 0$. Now, suppose that $n > 0$. Let $n = a + b$. By the induction hypothesis, $6a = 0$ and $6b = 0$. Therefore,

$$6n = 6(a+b) = 6a + 6b = 0 + 0 = 0.$$

66. ☞ What is wrong with the following reasoning? We show that for every $n \geq 3$, F_n is even. The base of the induction is trivial, since $F_3 = 2$. Now suppose that $n \geq 4$ and that F_m is even for all $m < n$. Then $F_n = F_{n-1} + F_{n-2}$, and by the induction hypothesis F_{n-1} and F_{n-2} are even. Thus, F_n is the sum of two even numbers, and must therefore be even.

2.10 GRAPHS

A *graph* is an ordered pair $G = (V, E)$, where V is a finite set and $E \subseteq V \times V$. The elements of V are called *nodes* or *vertices*, and the elements of E are called *edges*. We will follow the normal conventions of using n for the number of nodes and e for the number of edges. Where convenient we will take $V = \{v_2, v_2, \ldots, v_n\}$.

67. ☞ ☺☞ Prove by induction that a graph with n vertices can have at most $n(n-1)/2$ edges.

68. ☞ ☞ A *tournament* is a directed graph formed by taking the complete undirected graph and assigning arbitrary directions on the edges. That is, it is a graph $G = (V, E)$ such that for all $u, v \in V$, either exactly one of $(u, v), (v, u) \in E$. Show that every tournament has a Hamiltonian path, that is, a path that visits every vertex exactly once.

69. ☞ ⚙ ☺☞ An *Eulerian cycle* in a connected graph is a cycle in which every edge appears exactly once. Prove by induction that every graph in which each vertex has even degree (that is, each vertex has an even number of edges incident with it) has an Eulerian cycle.

The *hypercube* of *dimension* n is a graph defined as follows. A hypercube of dimension 0 is a single vertex. To build a hypercube of dimension n, start with a hypercube of dimension $n - 1$. Take a second, exact copy of this hypercube. Draw an edge from each vertex in the first copy to the corresponding vertex of the second copy. For example, Figure 2.5 shows the hypercubes of dimensions 0, 1, 2, 3, and 4.

70. ☞ Prove by induction that a hypercube of dimension n has 2^n vertices.

71. ☞ Prove by induction that a hypercube of dimension n has $n2^{n-1}$ edges.

72. ☞ Prove by induction that every hypercube has a Hamiltonian cycle, that is, a cycle that visits every vertex exactly once.

73. ☞ Prove by induction that the vertices of a hypercube can be colored using two colors so that no pair of adjacent vertices have the same color.

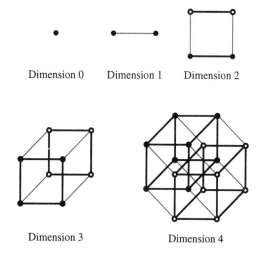

Dimension 0   Dimension 1   Dimension 2

Dimension 3   Dimension 4

Figure 2.5. Some hypercubes of various dimensions.

74. Prove by induction that the edges of an n-dimensional hypercube can be colored using n colors so that no pair of edges that share a common vertex have the same color.

75. Prove by induction that an n-dimensional hypercube has exactly

$$\binom{n}{k} 2^{n-k}$$

different subcubes of dimension k.

2.11 TREES

A *tree* is a special kind of graph defined as follows[1]. A single vertex v is a tree with root v. Suppose $T_i = (V_i, E_i)$ are disjoint trees with roots r_i respectively, for $1 \le i \le k$. Suppose $r \notin V_1, V_2, \ldots, V_k$. Then, $T = (V, E)$ is a tree, where

$$
\begin{aligned}
V &= V_1 \cup V_2 \cup \cdots \cup V_k \cup \{r\}, \\
E &= E_1 \cup E_2 \cup \cdots \cup E_k \cup \{(r, r_1), (r, r_2), \ldots, (r, r_k)\}.
\end{aligned}
$$

[1]Technically, this is actually called a *rooted tree*, but the distinction is not of prime importance here.

The root of a tree is said to be at level 1. For all $i \geq 1$, a child of a level i node is said to be at *level $i+1$*. The *number of levels* in a tree is the largest level number of any node in the tree. A *binary tree* is a tree in which all nodes have at most two children. A *complete binary tree* is a binary tree in which all leaves are at the same level.

76. ☞ Prove by induction that a tree with n vertices has exactly $n-1$ edges.

77. ☞ Prove by induction that a complete binary tree with n levels has $2^n - 1$ vertices.

78. ☞ Prove by induction that if there exists an n-node tree in which all the nonleaf nodes have k children, then $n \bmod k = 1$.

79. ☞ Prove by induction that for every n such that $n \bmod k = 1$, there exists an n-node tree in which all of the nonleaf nodes have k children.

80. ☞ Prove by induction that between any pair of vertices in a tree there is a unique path.

81. ☞ ☺♫ A *cycle* in a graph $G = (V, E)$ is a sequence of distinct vertices $v_1, v_2, \ldots, v_k$ such that $(v_k, v_1) \in E$, and for all $1 \leq i < k$, $(v_i, v_{i+1}) \in E$. Prove by induction that a tree is a connected graph that has no cycles.

82. ☞ ☺♫ Prove by induction that a connected graph that has no cycles is a tree.

83. ☞ A *spanning tree* of a graph $G = (V, E)$ is a tree $T = (V, F)$, where $F \subseteq E$. Prove by induction that an n-node graph can have as many as $(n-1)!$ spanning trees.

2.12 GEOMETRY

84. ☞ ☞ Prove that any set of regions defined by n lines in the plane can be colored with two colors so that no two regions that share an edge have the same color.

85. ☞ ☞ ☀ Prove by induction that n circles divide the plane into $n^2 - n + 2$ regions if every pair of circles intersect in exactly two points, and no three circles intersect in a common point. Does this hold for closed shapes other than circles?

86. ☞ ☀ A polygon is *convex* if every pair of points in the polygon can be joined by a straight line that lies in the polygon. Prove by induction on $n \geq 3$ that the sum of the angles of an n-vertex convex polygon is $180(n-2)$ degrees.

87. ☞ Consider any arrangement of $n \geq 3$ lines in general position in the plane (that is, no pair of lines is parallel, and no three lines can have a common point). Prove that at least one of the minimal connected regions that they form is a triangle.

88. ☞☞ Consider any arrangement of $n \geq 3$ lines in general position in the plane. Prove that at least $n - 2$ of the minimal connected regions in any such arrangement are triangles. Is this bound tight?

89. ☞ Prove that n straight lines in the plane, all passing through a single point, divide the plane into $2n$ regions.

90. ☞☞ Prove that n planes in space, all passing through a single point, no three of which meet in a straight line, divide space into $n(n - 2) + 2$ regions.

2.13   MISCELLANEOUS

91. ☞ Suppose M_i is an $r_{i-1} \times r_i$ matrix, for $1 \leq i \leq n$. Prove by induction on $n \geq 1$ that the matrix product $M_1 \cdot M_2 \cdots M_n$ is an $r_0 \times r_n$ matrix.

92. ☞ ☀ Prove by induction on $n \geq 1$ that the binary representation of n has $\lfloor \log n \rfloor + 1$ bits.

93. ☞ If $x, y \in \{\texttt{true}, \texttt{false}\}$, let $x \oplus y$ denote the exclusive-or of x and y, which is defined to be $\texttt{true}$ iff exactly one of x and y is $\texttt{true}$. Note that the exclusive-or operation is associative, that is, $a \oplus (b \oplus c) = (a \oplus b) \oplus c$. Prove by induction on n that $x_1 \oplus x_2 \oplus \cdots \oplus x_n$ is $\texttt{true}$ iff an odd number of $x_1, x_2, \ldots, x_n$ are $\texttt{true}$.

94. ☞ ☺☞ (The Pigeonhole Principle) Suppose n pigeons roost in m holes. Prove by induction on n that there must be at least one hole containing at least $\lceil n/m \rceil$ pigeons.

95. ☞☞ ☺☞ Suppose $A_n = \{a_1, a_2, \ldots, a_n\}$ is a set of distinct coin types, where each $a_i \in \mathbf{N}$, for $1 \leq i \leq n$. Suppose also that $a_1 \leq a_2 \leq \cdots \leq a_n$. The coin-changing problem is defined as follows. Given $C \in \mathbf{N}$, find the smallest number of coins from A_n that add up to C, given that an unlimited number of coins of each type are available. Show that for all $n \geq 2$, if $a_1 = 1$, then there is always a solution to the coin-changing problem, and that solution uses less than a_2 coins of type a_1. What happens when $a_1 \neq 1$?

A *Gray code* is a list of the 2^n n-bit strings in which each string differs from the previous one in exactly one bit. Consider the following algorithm for listing the

n-bit strings. If $n = 1$, the list is $0, 1$. If $n > 1$, first take the list of $(n-1)$-bit strings, and place a 0 in front of each string. Then, take a second copy of the list of $(n-1)$-bit strings, place a 1 in front of each string, reverse the order of the strings, and place it after the first list. So, for example, for $n = 2$ the list is $00, 01, 11, 10$, and for $n = 3$ the list is $000, 001, 011, 010, 110, 111, 101, 100$.

96. ☞ Show that every n-bit string appears exactly once in the list generated by the algorithm.

97. ☞ Show that the list has the Gray code property, that is, that each string differs from the previous one in exactly one bit.

2.14   HINTS

37. You will need to use strong induction. And your base case may not be what you expect at first,

48. Try combining four $n/2 \times n/2$ tours into one. Your induction hypothesis must be stronger than what you really need to prove — the tours you build must have some extra structure to allow them to be joined at the corners.

49. Look carefully at the example given before the problem. It illustrates the technique that you will need. Also, consider the hint to Problem 48.

53. You will need to use strong induction here.

57. You will need to use the identity

$$\binom{n}{r} = \binom{n-1}{r} + \binom{n-1}{r-1}.$$

(Can you prove this identity?) Be careful how you apply this identity (it doesn't always hold), and take special care with the upper and lower limits of the summation.

69. First, prove that any graph in which all vertices have even degree must have a cycle C (try constructing one). Delete C, leaving a smaller graph in which all vertices have even degree. Apply the induction hypothesis (careful: there is something I am not telling you). Put together C and the results of applying the induction hypothesis to give the Eulerian cycle.

85. The circles are a red herring.

86. The hardest part of this is the base case, proving that the sum of the three angles of a triangle is 180 degrees. It can be proved as follows. First, prove

it for a right-angled triangle (using symmetry). This can be extended to any triangle by judicious choice of diagonal. Once you have mastered the base case, the inductive step should be obvious.

92. You'll need to make two cases in your inductive step, according to whether n is a power of 2 (or something like that) or not.

2.15 SOLUTIONS

1. We are required to prove that for all $n \geq 0$, $\sum_{i=1}^{n} i = n(n+1)/2$. The claim is certainly true for $n = 0$, in which case both sides of the equation are zero. Suppose that $n \geq 0$ and $\sum_{i=1}^{n} i = n(n+1)/2$. We are required to prove that $\sum_{i=1}^{n+1} i = (n+1)(n+2)/2$. Now,

$$
\begin{aligned}
\sum_{i=1}^{n+1} i &= \sum_{i=1}^{n} i + (n+1) \\
&= n(n+1)/2 + (n+1) \qquad \text{(by the induction hypothesis)} \\
&= (n+1)(n+2)/2,
\end{aligned}
$$

as required.

8. We are required to prove that for all $n \geq 1$, $\sum_{i=1}^{n} 1/2^i = 1 - 1/2^n$. The claim is true for $n = 1$, since in this case both sides of the equation are equal to $1/2$. Now suppose that $n \geq 1$, and $\sum_{i=1}^{n} 1/2^i = 1 - 1/2^n$. It remains to prove that $\sum_{i=1}^{n+1} 1/2^i = 1 - 1/2^{n+1}$.

$$
\begin{aligned}
\sum_{i=1}^{n+1} 1/2^i &= \frac{1}{2} + \frac{1}{4} + \frac{1}{8} + \cdots + \frac{1}{2^{n+1}} \\
&= \frac{1}{2} + \frac{1}{2}\left(\frac{1}{2} + \frac{1}{4} + \frac{1}{8} + \cdots + \frac{1}{2^n}\right) \\
&= \frac{1}{2} + \frac{1}{2}\sum_{i=1}^{n}\frac{1}{2^i} \\
&- \frac{1}{2} + \frac{1}{2}\cdot\left(1 - \frac{1}{2^n}\right) \qquad \text{(by the induction hypothesis)} \\
&= 1 - 1/2^{n+1},
\end{aligned}
$$

as required.

11. We are required to prove that for all $n \geq 0$, $\sum_{i=0}^{n} 2^i = 2^{n+1} - 1$. The claim is certainly true for $n = 0$, in which case $\sum_{i=0}^{0} 2^i = 1 = 2^1 - 1$. Suppose that $n \geq 0$ and $\sum_{i=0}^{n} 2^i = 2^{n+1} - 1$. We are required to prove that

$\sum_{i=0}^{n+1} 2^i = 2^{n+2} - 1$. Now,

$$
\begin{aligned}
\sum_{i=0}^{n+1} 2^i &= \sum_{i=0}^{n} 2^i + 2^{n+1} \\
&= (2^{n+1} - 1) + 2^{n+1} \quad \text{(by the induction hypothesis)} \\
&= 2^{n+2} - 1,
\end{aligned}
$$

as required.

27. We are required to prove by induction on $n \geq 0$ that $n^3 + 2n$ is divisible by 3. The claim is true for $n = 0$, since then $n^3 + 2n = 0$, which is certainly divisible by 3. Suppose that $n \geq 0$, and $n^3 + 2n$ is divisible by 3. We are required to prove that $(n+1)^3 + 2(n+1)$ is divisible by 3. Now,

$$
\begin{aligned}
(n+1)^3 + 2(n+1) &= (n^3 + 3n^2 + 3n + 1) + (2n + 2) \\
&= n^3 + 3n^2 + 5n + 3 \\
&= (n^3 + 2n) + (3n^2 + 3n + 3).
\end{aligned}
$$

Since the first term is divisible by 3 (by the induction hypothesis) and the second term is obviously divisible by 3, it follows that $(n+1)^3 + 2(n+1)$ is divisible by 3, as required.

37. We are required to show that any amount of postage that is a positive integer number of cents $n > 7$ can be formed by using only 3-cent and 5-cent stamps. The claim is certainly true for $n = 8$ (one 3-cent and one 5-cent stamp), $n = 9$ (three 3-cent stamps), and $n = 10$ (two 5-cent stamps). Now suppose that $n \geq 11$ and all values up to $n - 1$ cents can be made with 3-cent and 5-cent stamps. Since $n \geq 11$, $n - 3 \geq 8$, and hence by hypothesis, $n - 3$ cents can be made with 3-cent and 5-cent stamps. Simply add a 3-cent stamp to this to make n cents. Notice that we can prove something stronger with just a little more work. The required postage can always be made using at most two 5-cent stamps. Can you prove this?

52. We are required to prove that for all $n \geq 0$, $\sum_{i=0}^{n} F_i = F_{n+2} - 1$. The claim is certainly true for $n = 0$, since the left-hand side of the equation is $F_0 = 0$, and the right-hand side is $F_2 - 1 = 1 - 1 = 0$. Now suppose that $n \geq 1$, and that $\sum_{i=0}^{n-1} F_i = F_{n+1} - 1$. Then,

$$
\begin{aligned}
\sum_{i=0}^{n} F_i &= \sum_{i=0}^{n-1} F_i + F_n \\
&= (F_{n+1} - 1) + F_n \quad \text{(by the induction hypothesis)} \\
&= F_{n+2} - 1,
\end{aligned}
$$

as required.

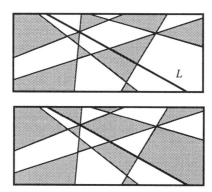

Figure 2.6. Shading the regions formed by all lines except
L (top), and the new shading obtained by flipping the colors
on one side of L (bottom).

84.   We are required to prove that any set of regions defined by n lines in the
plane can be colored with only two colors so that no two regions that share
an edge have the same color. The hypothesis is true for $n = 1$ (color one side
light, the other side dark). Now suppose that the hypothesis is true for n
lines. Suppose we are given $n + 1$ lines in the plane. Remove one of the lines
L, and color the remaining regions with two colors (which can be done, by
the induction hypothesis). Replace L. Reverse all of the colors on one side
of the line. Consider two regions that have a line in common. If that line is
not L, then by the induction hypothesis, the two regions have different colors
(either the same as before or reversed). If that line is L, then the two regions
formed a single region before L was replaced. Since we reversed colors on one
side of L only, they now have different colors.

2.16   COMMENTS

1.   This identity was apparently discovered by Gauss at age 9 in 1786. There is
an apocryphal story attached to this discovery. Gauss' teacher set the class
to add the numbers $1 + 2 + \cdots + 100$. One account I have heard said that the
teacher was lazy, and wanted to occupy the students for a long time so that
he could read a book. Another said that it was punishment for the class being
unruly and disruptive. Gauss came to the teacher within a few minutes with
an answer of 5050. The teacher was dismayed, and started to add. Some time
later, after some fretting and fuming, he came up with the wrong answer. He
refused to believe that he was wrong until Gauss explained:

$$\begin{array}{ccccccccc} & 1 & + & 2 & + & \cdots & + & 50 \\ + & 100 & + & 99 & + & \cdots & + & 51 \\ \hline & 101 & + & 101 & + & \cdots & + & 101 & = 50 \times 101 = 5050. \end{array}$$

Can you prove this result without using induction? The case for even n can easily be inferred from Gauss' example. The case for odd n is similar.

3. I could go on asking for more identities like this. I can never remember the exact form of the solution. Fortunately, there is not much need to. In general, if you are asked to solve

$$\sum_{i=1}^{n} i^k$$

for some $k \geq 1$, just remember that the solution is a polynomial in n with largest exponent $k+1$ (see Problem 21). Simply hypothesize that the sum is

$$a_{k+1} n^{k+1} + a_k n^k + \cdots + a_1 n + a_0$$

for some choice of $a_i \in \mathbf{R}$, $0 \leq i \leq k+1$, and try to prove it by induction. The right values for the constants will drop right out of the proof. It gets a bit tricky as k becomes larger, though. If you want to practice this technique, start with $k = 2$. If you want a challenge to your ability to do arithmetic, try $k = 4$.

4. Yes, I realize that you can solve this without induction by applying some elementary algebra and the identities of Problems 1 and 2. What I want you to do is practice your induction by proving this identity from first principles.

5. See the comment to Problem 4.

6. See the comment to Problem 4.

9. There is an elegant noninductive proof of this that you should have met in high school. Let $S = \sum_{i=0}^{n} a^i$. Then,

$$aS - S = \sum_{i=1}^{n+1} a^i - \sum_{i=0}^{n} a^i = a^{n+1} - 1.$$

Hence, $S = (a^{n+1} - 1)/(a - 1)$, as required.

10. This can also be solved by applying the identity of Problem 9 twice.

11. This is a special case of the identity in Problem 9. There is an easy noninductive proof of this fact that appeals more to computer science students than math students. The binary representation of $\sum_{i=0}^{n} 2^i$ is a string of $n+1$ ones, that is,

$$\underbrace{11\cdots1}_{n+1}.$$

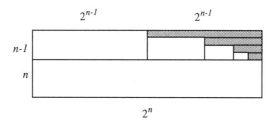

Figure 2.7. Using the method of areas to show that $\sum_{i=1}^{n} i2^i = (2n-1)2^n - \sum_{i=1}^{n-1} 2^i$.

If you add 1 to this, you get, in binary,

$$1\underbrace{00\cdots0}_{n+1},$$

that is, 2^{n+1}. Therefore, $\sum_{i=0}^{n} 2^i + 1 = 2^{n+1}$ or, equivalently, $\sum_{i=0}^{n} 2^i = 2^{n+1} - 1$.

13. There is an elegant noninductive proof of this using the *method of areas*. This technique works well for sums of products: Simply make a rectangle with area equal to each term of the sum, fit them together to "nearly" make a rectangle, and analyze the missing area.

$$
\begin{aligned}
\sum_{i=1}^{n} i2^i &= (2n-1)2^n - \sum_{i=1}^{n-1} 2^i \quad \text{(see Figure 2.7)}\\
&= (2n-1)2^n - (2^n - 2) \quad \text{(by Problem 1)}\\
&= (n-1)2^{n+1} + 2.
\end{aligned}
$$

15. This can also be solved using the method of areas sketched in the comment to Problem 13.

16. This can also be solved using algebra and the identity from Problem 15.

19. And, therefore, $3^n = O(n!)$. But we're getting ahead of ourselves here. See Chapter 3.

20. And, therefore, $2^n = \Omega(n^2)$. But we're getting ahead of ourselves here. See Chapter 3.

48. There are actually closed knight's tours on $n \times n$ chessboards for all even $n \geq 6$ (see Problem 369). Note that Problem 47 implies that there can be no such tour for odd n. The formal study of the knight's tour problem is said

to have begun with Euler [25] in 1759, who considered the standard 8×8 chessboard. Rouse Ball and Coxeter [8] give an interesting bibliography of the history of the problem from this point.

51. This problem was suggested to the author by Nainan Kovoor in 1990.

60. Don't cheat by using Stirling's approximation. You're supposed to be practicing your induction!

61. See the comment for Problem 60.

62. There is an elegant noninductive proof of the identity

$$\sum_{i=0}^{n} i \cdot \binom{n}{i} = n2^{n-1}.$$

Write down every string of n bits. Since there are $\binom{n}{i}$ strings with exactly i ones, you must have written exactly

$$\sum_{i=0}^{n} i \cdot \binom{n}{i}$$

ones. But since you have written exactly as many ones as zeros, and you have written $n2^n$ bits in all, there must be $n2^{n-1}$ ones.

64. Of course it is obvious that the proof is wrong, since all horses are not of the same color. What I want you to do is point out *where* in the proof is there a false statement made?

67. This can be proved using Problem 1, but what I'm looking for is a straight-forward inductive proof.

69. An Eulerian cycle is not possible if the graph has at least one vertex of odd degree. (Can you prove this?) Therefore, we conclude that a graph has a Eulerian cycle iff it is connected and all vertices have even degree. The Swiss mathematician Leonhard Euler first proved this in 1736 [24].

81. This problem together with Problem 82 show that "a connected graph with no cycles" is an alternate definition of a tree. You'll see this in the literature as often as you'll see the recursive definition given at the beginning of Section 2.11.

82. See the comment for Problem 81.

94. Yes, this is a little contrived. It's easier to prove by contradiction. But it's good practice in using induction.

95. See also Problems 415 and 471.

Chapter 3

Big-O and Big-Ω

Big-O notation is useful for the analysis of algorithms since it captures the asymptotic growth pattern of functions and ignores the constant multiple (which is out of our control anyway when algorithms are translated into programs). We will use the following definitions (although alternatives exist; see Section 3.5). Suppose that $f, g : \mathbb{N} \to \mathbb{N}$.

- $f(n)$ is $O(g(n))$ if there exists $c, n_0 \in \mathbb{R}^+$ such that for all $n \geq n_0$, $f(n) \leq c \cdot g(n)$.
- $f(n)$ is $\Omega(g(n))$ if there exists $c, n_0 \in \mathbb{R}^+$ such that for all $n \geq n_0$, $f(n) \geq c \cdot g(n)$.
- $f(n)$ is $\Theta(g(n))$ if $f(n)$ is $O(g(n))$ and $f(n)$ is $\Omega(g(n))$.
- $f(n)$ is $o(g(n))$ if $\lim_{n \to \infty} f(n)/g(n) = 0$.
- $f(n)$ is $\omega(g(n))$ if $\lim_{n \to \infty} g(n)/f(n) = 0$.
- $f(n) \sim g(n)$ if $\lim_{n \to \infty} f(n)/g(n) = 1$.

We will follow the normal convention of writing, for example, "$f(n) = O(g(n))$" instead of "$f(n)$ is $O(g(n))$", even though the equality sign does not indicate true equality. The proper definition of "$O(g(n))$" is as a set:

$$O(g(n)) = \{f(n) \mid \text{there exists } c, n_0 \in \mathbb{R}^+ \text{ such that for all } n \geq n_0, \ f(n) \leq c \cdot g(n)\}.$$

Then, "$f(n) = O(g(n))$" can be interpreted as meaning "$f(n) \in O(g(n))$."

3.1 RANK THE FUNCTIONS

98. ☞ ☼ Consider the following eighteen functions:

$\sqrt{n}$	n	2^n
$n \log n$	$n - n^3 + 7n^5$	$n^2 + \log n$
n^2	n^3	$\log n$
$n^{1/3} + \log n$	$(\log n)^2$	$n!$
$\ln n$	$n/\log n$	$\log \log n$
$(1/3)^n$	$(3/2)^n$	6

Group these functions so that $f(n)$ and $g(n)$ are in the same group if and only if $f(n) = O(g(n))$ and $g(n) = O(f(n))$, and list the groups in increasing order.

99. ☞ ☼ Draw a line from each of the five functions in the center to the best big-Ω value on the left, and the best big-O value on the right.

$\Omega(1/n)$		$O(1/n)$
$\Omega(1)$		$O(1)$
$\Omega(\log\log n)$		$O(\log\log n)$
$\Omega(\log n)$		$O(\log n)$
$\Omega(\log^2 n)$		$O(\log^2 n)$
$\Omega(\sqrt[3]{n})$		$O(\sqrt[3]{n})$
$\Omega(n/\log n)$	$1/(\log n)$	$O(n/\log n)$
$\Omega(n)$	$7n^5 - 3n + 2$	$O(n)$
$\Omega(n^{1.00001})$	$(n^2+n)/(\log^2 n + \log n)$	$O(n^{1.00001})$
$\Omega(n^2/\log^2 n)$	$2^{\log^2 n}$	$O(n^2/\log^2 n)$
$\Omega(n^2/\log n)$	3^n	$O(n^2/\log n)$
$\Omega(n^2)$		$O(n^2)$
$\Omega(n^{3/2})$		$O(n^{3/2})$
$\Omega(2^n)$		$O(2^n)$
$\Omega(5^n)$		$O(5^n)$
$\Omega(n^n)$		$O(n^n)$
$\Omega(n^{n^2})$		$O(n^{n^2})$

For each of the following pairs of functions $f(n)$ and $g(n)$, either $f(n) = O(g(n))$ or $g(n) = O(f(n))$, but not both. Determine which is the case.

100. ☞ $f(n) = (n^2 - n)/2$, $g(n) = 6n$.

101. ☞ $f(n) = n + 2\sqrt{n}$, $g(n) = n^2$.

102. ☞ $f(n) = n + \log n$, $g(n) = n\sqrt{n}$.

103. ☞ $f(n) = n^2 + 3n + 4$, $g(n) = n^3$.

104. ☞ $f(n) = n\log n$, $g(n) = n\sqrt{n}/2$.

105. ☞ $f(n) = n + \log n$, $g(n) = \sqrt{n}$.

106. ☞ $f(n) = 2(\log n)^2$, $g(n) = \log n + 1$.

107. ☞ $f(n) = 4n\log n + n$, $g(n) = (n^2 - n)/2$.

3.2   TRUE OR FALSE?

108. ☞ $n^2 = O(n^3)$.

109. ☞ $n^3 = O(n^2)$.

110. ☞ $2n^2 + 1 = O(n^2)$.

111. ☞ $n \log n = O(n\sqrt{n})$.

112. ☞ $\sqrt{n} = O(\log n)$.

113. ☞ $\log n = O(\sqrt{n})$.

114. ☞ $n^3 = O(n^2(1 + n^2))$.

115. ☞ $n^2(1 + \sqrt{n}) = O(n^2)$.

116. ☞ $n^2(1 + \sqrt{n}) = O(n^2 \log n)$.

117. ☞ $3n^2 + \sqrt{n} = O(n^2)$.

118. ☞ $3n^2 + \sqrt{n} = O(n + n\sqrt{n} + \sqrt{n})$.

119. ☞ $\log n + \sqrt{n} = O(n)$.

120. ☞ $\sqrt{n} \log n = O(n)$.

121. ☞ $1/n = O(\log n)$.

122. ☞ $\log n = O(1/n)$.

123. ☞ $\log n = O(n^{-1/2})$.

124. ☞ $n + \sqrt{n} = O(\sqrt{n} \log n)$.

125. ☞ If $f(n) \sim g(n)$, then $f(n) = \Theta(g(n))$.

126. ☞ If $f(n) = \Theta(g(n))$, then $g(n) = \Theta(f(n))$.

For each of the following pairs of functions $f(n)$ and $g(n)$, state whether $f(n) = O(g(n))$, $f(n) = \Omega(g(n))$, $f(n) = \Theta(g(n))$, or none of the above.

127. ☞ $f(n) = n^2 + 3n + 4$, $g(n) = 6n + 7$.

128. ☞ $f(n) = \sqrt{n}$, $g(n) = \log(n + 3)$.

129. ☞ $f(n) = n\sqrt{n}$, $g(n) = n^2 - n$.

130. ☞ $f(n) = n + n\sqrt{n}$, $g(n) = 4n \log(n^2 + 1)$.

131. ☞ $f(n) = (n^2 + 2)/(1 + 2^{-n})$, $g(n) = n + 3$.

132. ☞ $f(n) = 2^n - n^2$, $g(n) = n^4 + n^2$.

3.3 PROVING BIG-O

133.   Prove that $(n+1)^2 = O(n^2)$.

134.   Prove that $3n^2 - 8n + 9 = O(n^2)$.

135.   Prove that for all $k \geq 1$ and all $a_k, a_{k-1}, \ldots, a_1, a_0 \in \mathbf{R}$,

$$a_k n^k + a_{k-1} n^{k-1} + \cdots + a_1 n + a_0 = O(n^k).$$

136.   Prove that $\lceil \log n \rceil = O(n)$.

137.   Prove that $3n \lfloor \log n \rfloor = O(n^2)$.

138.   Prove that $n^2 - 3n - 18 = \Omega(n)$.

139.   Prove that $n^3 - 3n^2 - n + 1 = \Theta(n^3)$.

140.   Prove that $n = O(2^n)$.

141.   Prove that $2n + 1 = O(2^n)$.

142.   Prove that $9999n + 635 = O(2^n)$.

143.   Prove that $cn + d = O(2^n)$ for all $c, d \in \mathbf{R}^+$.

144.   Prove that $n^2 = O(2^n)$.

145.   Prove that $cn^2 + d = O(2^n)$ for all $c, d \in \mathbf{R}^+$.

146.   Prove that $cn^k + d = O(2^n)$ for all $c, d, k \in \mathbf{R}^+$.

147.   Prove that $2^n = O(n!)$.

148.   Prove that $n! = \Omega(2^n)$.

149.   Does $n^{\log n} = O((\log n)^n)$? Prove your answer.

150.   Does $n^{\log n} = \Omega((\log n)^n)$? Prove your answer.

151.   Does $n^{\log \log \log n} = O((\log n)!)$? Prove your answer.

152.   Does $n^{\log \log \log n} = \Omega((\log n)!)$? Prove your answer.

153.   Does $(n!)! = O(((n-1)!)!(n-1)!^{n!})$? Prove your answer.

154.   Does $(n!)! = \Omega(((n-1)!)!(n-1)!^{n!})$? Prove your answer.

155.   Prove or disprove:

$$O\left(\left(\frac{n^2}{\log \log n}\right)^{1/2}\right) = O(\lfloor \sqrt{n} \rfloor).$$

156. 🎓🎓 Prove or disprove: $2^{(1+O(1/n))^2} = 2 + O(1/n)$.

Compare the following pairs of functions f, g. In each case, say whether $f = o(g)$, $f = \omega(g)$, or $f = \Theta(g)$, and prove your claim.

157. 🎓 $f(n) = 100n + \log n$, $g(n) = n + (\log n)^2$.

158. 🎓 $f(n) = \log n$, $g(n) = \log \log(n^2)$.

159. 🎓 $f(n) = n^2/\log n$, $g(n) = n(\log n)^2$.

160. 🎓🎓 $f(n) = (\log n)^{10^6}$, $g(n) = n^{10^{-6}}$.

161. 🎓🎓 $f(n) = n \log n$, $g(n) = (\log n)^{\log n}$.

162. 🎓 $f(n) = n2^n$, $g(n) = 3^n$.

For each of the following pairs of functions $f(n)$ and $g(n)$, find $c \in \mathbf{R}^+$ such that $f(n) \le c \cdot g(n)$ for all $n > 1$.

163. 🎓 $f(n) = n^2 + n$, $g(n) = n^2$.

164. 🎓 $f(n) = 2\sqrt{n} + 1$, $g(n) = n + n^2$.

165. 🎓 $f(n) = n^2 + n + 1$, $g(n) = 2n^3$.

166. 🎓 $f(n) = n\sqrt{n} + n^2$, $g(n) = n^2$.

167. 🎓 $f(n) = 12n + 3$, $g(n) = 2n - 1$.

168. 🎓 $f(n) = n^2 - n + 1$, $g(n) = n^2/2$.

169. 🎓 $f(n) = 5n + 1$, $g(n) = (n^2 - 6n)/2$.

170. 🎓 $f(n) = 5\lfloor\sqrt{n}\rfloor - 1$, $g(n) = n - \lceil\sqrt{n}\rceil$.

3.4   MANIPULATING BIG-O

171. 🎓 💡 ☞ Prove that if $f_1(n) = O(g_1(n))$ and $f_2(n) = O(g_2(n))$, then $f_1(n) + f_2(n) = O(g_1(n) + g_2(n))$.

172. 🎓 Prove that if $f_1(n) = \Omega(g_1(n))$ and $f_2(n) = \Omega(g_2(n))$, then $f_1(n) + f_2(n) = \Omega(g_1(n) + g_2(n))$.

173. 🎓 ☺ Prove that if $f_1(n) = O(g_1(n))$ and $f_2(n) = O(g_2(n))$, then $f_1(n) + f_2(n) = O(\max\{g_1(n), g_2(n)\})$.

174. ☞ Prove that if $f_1(n) = \Omega(g_1(n))$ and $f_2(n) = \Omega(g_2(n))$, then $f_1(n) + f_2(n) = \Omega(\min\{g_1(n), g_2(n)\})$.

175. ☞ Suppose that $f_1(n) = \Theta(g_1(n))$ and $f_2(n) = \Theta(g_2(n))$. Is it true that $f_1(n) + f_2(n) = \Theta(g_1(n) + g_2(n))$? Is it true that $f_1(n) + f_2(n) = \Theta(\max\{g_1(n), g_2(n)\})$? Is it true that $f_1(n) + f_2(n) = \Theta(\min\{g_1(n), g_2(n)\})$? Justify your answer.

176. ☞ ☺☞ Prove that if $f_1(n) = O(g_1(n))$ and $f_2(n) = O(g_2(n))$, then $f_1(n) \cdot f_2(n) = O(g_1(n) \cdot g_2(n))$.

177. ☞ Prove that if $f_1(n) = \Omega(g_1(n))$ and $f_2(n) = \Omega(g_2(n))$, then $f_1(n) \cdot f_2(n) = \Omega(g_1(n) \cdot g_2(n))$.

178. ☞☞ Prove or disprove: For all functions $f(n)$ and $g(n)$, either $f(n) = O(g(n))$ or $g(n) = O(f(n))$.

179. ☞☞ Prove or disprove: If $f(n) > 0$ and $g(n) > 0$ for all n, then $O(f(n) + g(n)) = f(n) + O(g(n))$.

180. ☞☞ Prove or disprove: $O(f(n)^\alpha) = O(f(n))^\alpha$ for all $\alpha \in \mathbf{R}^+$.

181. ☞☞ Prove or disprove: $O(x + y)^2 = O(x^2) + O(y^2)$.

182. ☞ Multiply $\log n + 6 + O(1/n)$ by $n + O(\sqrt{n})$ and simplify your answer as much as possible.

183. ☞ Show that big-O is transitive. That is, if $f(n) = O(g(n))$ and $g(n) = O(h(n))$, then $f(n) = O(h(n))$.

184. ☞ Prove that if $f(n) = O(g(n))$, then $f(n)^k = O(g(n)^k)$.

185. ☞ Prove or disprove: If $f(n) = O(g(n))$, then $2^{f(n)} = O(2^{g(n)})$.

186. ☞ Prove or disprove: If $f(n) = O(g(n))$, then $\log f(n) = O(\log g(n))$.

187. ☞ Suppose $f(n) = \Theta(g(n))$. Prove that $h(n) = O(f(n))$ iff $h(n) = O(g(n))$.

188. ☞ Prove or disprove: If $f(n) = O(g(n))$, then $f(n)/h(n) = O(g(n)/h(n))$.

3.5   ALTERNATIVE DEFINITIONS

Here is an alternative definition of O.

- $f(n)$ is $O_1(g(n))$ if there exists $c \in \mathbf{R}$ such that $\lim_{n \to \infty} f(n)/g(n) = c$.

189. ☞ Prove that if $f(n) = O(g(n))$, then $f(n) = O_1(g(n))$, or find a counterexample to this claim.

190. ☞ Prove that if $f(n) = O_1(g(n))$, then $f(n) = O(g(n))$, or find a counterexample to this claim.

Here are two alternative definitions of Ω.

- $f(n)$ is $\Omega_1(g(n))$ if there exists $c \in \mathbf{R}^+$ such that for infinitely many n, $f(n) \geq c \cdot g(n)$.
- $f(n)$ is $\Omega_2(g(n))$ if there exists $c \in \mathbf{R}^+$ such that for all $n_0 \in \mathbf{N}$, there exists $n \geq n_0$ such that $f(n) \geq c \cdot g(n)$.

191. ☞ Prove that if $f(n) = \Omega(g(n))$, then $f(n) = \Omega_2(g(n))$, or find a counterexample to this claim.

192. ☞ ☞ Prove that if $f(n) = \Omega_2(g(n))$, then $f(n) = \Omega(g(n))$, or find a counterexample to this claim.

193. ☞ Prove that if $f(n) = \Omega_1(g(n))$, then $f(n) = \Omega_2(g(n))$, or find a counterexample to this claim.

194. ☞ Prove that if $f(n) = \Omega_2(g(n))$, then $f(n) = \Omega_1(g(n))$, or find a counterexample to this claim.

195. ☞ ☞ Prove or disprove: If $f(n) \neq O(g(n))$, then $f(n) = \Omega(g(n))$. If $f(n) \neq O(g(n))$, then $f(n) = \Omega_2(g(n))$.

196. ☞ ☞ Define the relation $\equiv$ by $f(n) \equiv g(n)$ iff $f(n) = \Omega(g(n))$ and $g(n) = \Omega(f(n))$. Similarly, define the relation $\equiv_2$ by $f(n) \equiv g(n)$ iff $f(n) = \Omega_2(g(n))$ and $g(n) = \Omega_2(f(n))$. Show that $\equiv$ is an equivalence relation, but $\equiv_2$ is not an equivalence relation.

3.6   FIND THE FUNCTIONS

Find two functions $f(n)$ and $g(n)$ that satisfy the following relationships. If no such f and g exist, write "None."

197. ☞ ☞ $f(n) = o(g(n))$ and $f(n) \neq \Theta(g(n))$.

198. ☞ ☞ $f(n) = \Theta(g(n))$ and $f(n) = o(g(n))$.

199. ☞ ☞ $f(n) = \Theta(g(n))$ and $f(n) \neq O(g(n))$.

200. ☞ ☞ $f(n) = \Omega(g(n))$ and $f(n) \neq O(g(n))$.

201. ☞ ☞ $f(n) = \Omega(g(n))$ and $f(n) \neq o(g(n))$.

3.7   HINTS

98. There are a lot of groups.

99. Be careful with $(n^2 + n)/(\log^2 n + \log n)$.

136. When solving problems that require you to prove that $f(n) = O(g(n))$, it is a good idea to try induction first. That is, pick a c and an n_0, and try to prove that for all $n \geq n_0$, $f(n) \leq c \cdot g(n)$. Try starting with $n_0 = 1$. A good way of guessing a value for c is to look at $f(n)$ and $g(n)$ for $n = n_0, \cdots, n_0 + 10$. If the first function seems to grow faster than the second, it means that you must adjust your n_0 higher — eventually (unless the thing you are trying to prove is false), the first function will grow more slowly than the second. The ratio of $f(n_0)/g(n_0)$ gives you your first cut for c. Don't be afraid to make c higher than this initial guess to help you make it easier to prove the inductive step. This happens quite often. You might even have to go back and adjust n_0 higher to make things work out correctly.

171. Start by writing down the definitions for $f_1(n) = O(g_1(n))$ and $f_2(n) = O(g_2(n))$.

3.8   SOLUTIONS

133. We are required to prove that $(n + 1)^2 = O(n^2)$. We need to find a constant c such that $(n + 1)^2 \leq cn^2$. That is, $n^2 + 2n + 1 \leq cn^2$ or, equivalently, $(c - 1)n^2 - 2n - 1 \geq 0$. Is this possible? It is if $c > 1$. Take $c = 4$. The roots of $3n^2 - 2n - 1$ are $(2 \pm \sqrt{4 + 12})/2 = \{-1/3, 1\}$. The second root gives us the correct value for n_0. Therefore, for all $n \geq 1$, $(n + 1)^2 \leq 4n^2$, and so by definition, $(n + 1)^2 = O(n^2)$.

136. We are required to prove that $\lceil \log n \rceil = O(n)$. By looking at $\lceil \log n \rceil$ for small values of n, it appears that for all $n \geq 1$, $\lceil \log n \rceil \leq n$. The proof is by induction on n. The claim is certainly true for $n = 1$. Now suppose that $n > 1$, and $\lceil \log(n - 1) \rceil \leq n - 1$. Then,

$$
\begin{aligned}
\lceil \log n \rceil &\leq \lceil \log(n - 1) \rceil + 1 \\
&\leq (n - 1) + 1 \quad \text{(by the induction hypothesis)} \\
&= n.
\end{aligned}
$$

Hence, we can take $c = 1$ and $n_0 = 1$.

137. We are required to prove that $3n\lfloor \log n \rfloor = O(n^2)$. By looking at $3n\lfloor \log n \rfloor$ for small values of n, it appears that for all $n \geq 1$, $3n\lfloor \log n \rfloor \leq 3n^2$. The proof is by induction on n. The claim is certainly true for $n = 1$. Now suppose that

$n > 1$, and $3(n-1)\lfloor \log(n-1) \rfloor \le 3(n-1)^2$. Then,

$$
\begin{aligned}
& 3n\lfloor \log n \rfloor \\
\le\ & 3n(\lfloor \log(n-1) \rfloor + 1) \\
=\ & 3(n-1)(\lfloor \log(n-1) \rfloor + 1) + 3(\lfloor \log(n-1) \rfloor + 1) \\
=\ & 3(n-1)\lfloor \log(n-1) \rfloor + 3(n-1) + 3(\lfloor \log(n-1) \rfloor + 1) \\
\le\ & 3(n-1)^2 + 3(n-1) + 3(\lfloor \log(n-1) \rfloor + 1) \\
& \text{(by the induction hypothesis)} \\
\le\ & 3(n-1)^2 + 3(n-1) + 3n \quad \text{(see the solution to Problem 136)} \\
=\ & 3n^2 - 6n + 3 + 3n - 3 + 3n \\
=\ & 3n^2.
\end{aligned}
$$

Hence, we can take $c = 3$ and $n_0 = 1$.

171. We are required to prove that if $f_1(n) = O(g_1(n))$ and $f_2(n) = O(g_2(n))$, then $f_1(n) + f_2(n) = O(g_1(n) + g_2(n))$. Suppose for all $n \ge n_1$, $f_1(n) \le c_1 \cdot g_1(n)$ and for all $n \ge n_2$, $f_2(n) \le c_2 \cdot g_2(n)$. Let $n_0 = \max\{n_1, n_2\}$ and $c_0 = \max\{c_1, c_2\}$. Then for all $n \ge n_0$, $f_1(n) + f_2(n) \le c_1 \cdot g_1(n) + c_2 \cdot g_2(n) \le c_0(g_1(n) + g_2(n))$.

3.9 COMMENTS

173. This is often called the *sum rule* for big-Os.

176. This is often called the *product rule* for big-Os.

Chapter 4

Recurrence Relations

Recurrence relations are a useful tool for the analysis of recursive algorithms, as we will see later in Section 6.2. The problems in this chapter are intended to develop skill in solving recurrence relations.

4.1 SIMPLE RECURRENCES

Solve the following recurrences exactly.

202. ☞ ✏ 📜 ☺☞ $T(1) = 1$, and for all $n \geq 2$, $T(n) = 3T(n-1) + 2$.

203. ☞ $T(1) = 8$, and for all $n \geq 2$, $T(n) = 3T(n-1) - 15$.

204. ☞ $T(1) = 2$, and for all $n \geq 2$, $T(n) = T(n-1) + n - 1$.

205. ☞ $T(1) = 3$, and for all $n \geq 2$, $T(n) = T(n-1) + 2n - 3$.

206. ☞ $T(1) = 1$, and for all $n \geq 2$, $T(n) = 2T(n-1) + n - 1$.

207. ☞ $T(1) = 5$, and for all $n \geq 2$, $T(n) = 2T(n-1) + 3n + 1$.

208. ☞ 📝 $T(1) = 1$, and for all $n \geq 2$ a power of 2, $T(n) = 2T(n/2) + 6n - 1$.

209. ☞ $T(1) = 4$, and for all $n \geq 2$ a power of 2, $T(n) = 2T(n/2) + 3n + 2$.

210. ☞ $T(1) = 1$, and for all $n \geq 2$ a power of 6, $T(n) = 6T(n/6) + 2n + 3$.

211. ☞ $T(1) = 3$, and for all $n \geq 2$ a power of 6, $T(n) = 6T(n/6) + 3n - 1$.

212. ☞ $T(1) = 3$, and for all $n \geq 2$ a power of 3, $T(n) = 4T(n/3) + 2n - 1$.

213. ☞ $T(1) = 2$, and for all $n \geq 2$ a power of 3, $T(n) = 4T(n/3) + 3n - 5$.

214. ☞ 📝 $T(1) = 1$, and for all $n \geq 2$ a power of 2, $T(n) = 3T(n/2) + n^2 - n$.

215. ☞ $T(1) = 4$, and for all $n \geq 2$ a power of 2, $T(n) = 3T(n/2) + n^2 - 2n + 1$.

216. ☞ $T(1) = 1$, and for all $n \geq 2$ a power of 2, $T(n) = 3T(n/2) + n - 2$.

217. ☞ $T(1) = 1$, and for all $n \geq 2$ a power of 2, $T(n) = 3T(n/2) + 5n - 7$.

218. ☞ $T(1) = 1$, and for all $n \geq 2$ a power of 3, $T(n) = 4T(n/3) + n^2$.

219. ☞ $T(1) = 1$, and for all $n \geq 2$ a power of 3, $T(n) = 4T(n/3) + n^2 - 7n + 5$.

220. ☞ $T(1) = 1$, and for $n \geq 4$ a power of 4, $T(n) = T(n/4) + \sqrt{n} + 1$.

4.2 MORE DIFFICULT RECURRENCES

221. ☞☞ Suppose $0 < \alpha, \beta < 1$, where $\alpha + \beta = 1$. Let $T(1) = 1$, and for all $n \geq 1$, $T(n) = T(\alpha n) + T(\beta n) + cn$, for some $c \in \mathbb{N}$. Prove that $T(n) = O(n \log n)$. You may make any necessary assumptions about n.

222. ☞☞ ☺☞ The Fibonacci numbers F_n for $n \geq 0$ are defined recursively as follows: $F_0 = 0$, $F_1 = 1$, and for $n \geq 2$, $F_n = F_{n-1} + F_{n-2}$. Prove by induction on n that $F_n = (\phi^n - \hat{\phi}^n)/\sqrt{5}$, where $\phi = (1 + \sqrt{5})/2$, and $\hat{\phi} = (1 - \sqrt{5})/2$.

Let $X(n)$ be the number of different ways of parenthesizing the product of n values. For example, $X(1) = X(2) = 1$, $X(3) = 2$ (they are $(xx)x$ and $x(xx)$), and $X(4) = 5$ (they are $x((xx)x)$, $x(x(xx))$, $(xx)(xx)$, $((xx)x)x$, and $(x(xx))x$).

223. ☞☞ Prove that if $n \leq 2$, then $X(n) = 1$; and otherwise

$$X(n) = \sum_{k=1}^{n-1} X(k) \cdot X(n-k)$$

224. ☞☞ 💡 Show that for all $n \geq 1$, $X(n) \geq 2^{n-2}$.

225. ☞☞☞ Show that

$$X(n) = \frac{1}{n} \binom{2n-2}{n-1}.$$

Solve the following recurrences exactly.

226. ☞☞ 💡 📝 $T(1) = 1$, $T(2) = 6$, and for all $n \geq 3$, $T(n) = T(n-2) + 3n + 4$.

227. ☞☞ $T(0) = c$, $T(1) = d$, and for $n > 1$, $T(n) = T(n-2) + n$.

228. ☞☞ $T(1) = 1$, $T(2) = 6$, $T(3) = 13$, and for all $n \geq 4$,

$$T(n) = T(n-3) + 5n - 9.$$

229. ☞☞ $T(1) = 1$, and for all $n \geq 2$, $T(n) = 2T(n-1) + n^2 - 2n + 1$.

230. ☞☞ $T(1) = 1$, and for all $n \geq 2$, $T(n) = n \cdot T(n-1) + n$.

4.3 GENERAL FORMULAE

It is normal to teach the general solution to recurrences of the form $T(n) = aT(n/c) + bn$ (see, for example, Aho, Hopcroft, and Ullman [1, Theorem 1.1]). The following are interesting variants of this recurrence.

231. ☞☞ State and prove a general formula for recurrences of the form

$$T(n) = \begin{cases} d & \text{if } n \le 1 \\ aT(n/c) + b & \text{otherwise.} \end{cases}$$

232. ☞☞ State and prove a general formula for recurrences of the form

$$T(n) = \begin{cases} d & \text{if } n \le 1 \\ aT(n/c) + bn^2 & \text{otherwise.} \end{cases}$$

233. ☞☞ State and prove a general formula for recurrences of the form

$$T(n) = \begin{cases} d & \text{if } n \le 1 \\ aT(n/c) + bn^k & \text{otherwise.} \end{cases}$$

234. ☞☞ Prove that the asymptotic solution of the recurrence relation

$$T(n) = \begin{cases} 0 & \text{if } 0 \le n < c \\ 2T(n - c) + k & \text{otherwise.} \end{cases}$$

where $c, k \in \mathbb{N}$, is $T(n) = \Theta(d^n)$ for some constant d.

4.4 RECURRENCES WITH FULL HISTORY

Solve the following recurrences exactly.

235. ☞ 📝 $T(1) = 1$, and for all $n \ge 2$,

$$T(n) = \sum_{i=1}^{n-1} T(i) + 1.$$

236. ☞ $T(1) = 1$, and for all $n \ge 2$,

$$T(n) = \sum_{i=1}^{n-1} T(i) + 7.$$

237. ☞ $T(1) = 1$, and for all $n \geq 2$,

$$T(n) = \sum_{i=1}^{n-1} T(i) + n^2.$$

238. ☞ $T(1) = 1$, and for all $n \geq 2$,

$$T(n) = 2\sum_{i=1}^{n-1} T(i) + 1.$$

239. ☞☞ $T(1) = 1$, and for all $n \geq 2$,

$$T(n) = \sum_{i=1}^{n-1} T(n - i) + 1.$$

240. ☞☞ $T(1) = 1$, and for all $n \geq 2$,

$$T(n) = \sum_{i=1}^{n-1} (T(i) + T(n - i)) + 1.$$

4.5 RECURRENCES WITH FLOORS AND CEILINGS

241. ☞☞ Suppose $T(1) = 1$, and for all $n \geq 2$, $T(n) = T(\lfloor n/2 \rfloor) + n - 1$. Show that $2n - \lfloor \log n \rfloor - 1 \leq T(n) \leq 2n - \lfloor \log n \rfloor /2 - 1$.

242. ☞☞ ☀ Suppose $T(1) = 1$, and for all $n \geq 2$, $T(n) = T(\lfloor n/2 \rfloor) + T(\lfloor n/2 \rfloor) + n - 1$. Find an exact solution for $T(n)$.

243. ☞☞ ☀ Solve the following recurrence relation exactly. $T(1) = 1$ and for all $n \geq 2$, $T(n) = T(\lfloor n/2 \rfloor) + 1$.

244. ☞☞ Solve the following recurrence relation exactly. $T(1) = 1$ and for all $n \geq 2$, $T(n) = T(\lceil n/2 \rceil) + 1$.

245. ☞☞ Solve the following recurrence relation exactly. $T(1) = 1$, and for $n \geq 2$, $T(n) = 2T(\lfloor n/2 \rfloor) + 6n - 1$.

246. ☞☞ Solve the following recurrence relation exactly. $T(1) = 2$, and for all $n \geq 2$, $T(n) = 4T(\lceil n/3 \rceil) + 3n - 5$.

247. ☞☞ Solve the following recurrence: $T(1) = 1$, and for all $n \geq 2$, $T(n) = T(\lfloor \sqrt{n} \rfloor) + 1$.

248. ☞☞☞ ☀ Solve the following recurrence: $T(1) = T(2) = 1$, and for all $n \geq 3$, $T(n) = T(\lfloor n/\log n \rfloor) + 1$.

4.6 HINTS

202. Try repeated substitution (see the comment to Problem 202 for a definition of this term).

224. Use induction on n. The base case will be $n \leq 4$.

226. If you think about it, this is really two independent recurrence relations, one for odd n and one for even n. Therefore, you will need to make a special case for even n and one for odd n. Once you realize this, the recurrences in this group of problems are fairly easy.

242. The solution is $T(n) = n\lceil \log n \rceil - 2^{\lceil \log n \rceil} + 1$. This can be proved by induction. Can you derive this answer from first principles?

243. This problem is difficult to solve directly, but it becomes easy when you use the following fact from Graham, Knuth, and and Patashnik [30, Section 6.6]. Suppose $f : \mathbf{R} \to \mathbf{R}$ is continuous and monotonically increasing, and has the property that if $f(x) \in \mathbf{Z}$, then $x \in \mathbf{Z}$. Then, $\lfloor f(\lfloor x \rfloor) \rfloor = \lfloor f(x) \rfloor$ and $\lceil f(\lceil x \rceil) \rceil = \lceil f(x) \rceil$.

248. The answer is that for $n \geq 3$, $T(n) \leq 1.76 \log n / \log \log n$, but this may not help you much.

4.7 SOLUTIONS

202. Suppose $T(1) = 1$, and for all $n \geq 2$, $T(n) = 3T(n-1) + 2$. If n is large enough, then by repeated substitution,

$$
\begin{aligned}
T(n) &= 3T(n-1) + 2 \quad \text{(after one substitution)} \\
&= 3(3T(n-2) + 2) + 2 \\
&= 9T(n-2) + 2 \cdot 3 + 2 \quad \text{(after two substitutions)} \\
&= 9(3T(n-3) + 2) + 2 \cdot 3 + 2 \\
&= 27T(n-3) + 2 \cdot 9 + 2 \cdot 3 + 2 \quad \text{(after three substitutions).}
\end{aligned}
$$

It looks like there's a pattern developing. After i substitutions,

$$
T(n) = 3^i T(n-i) + 2 \sum_{j=0}^{i-1} 3^j. \tag{4.1}
$$

We can prove that identity (4.1) is true by induction on i. It is trivially true for $i = 1$. Now suppose that $i > 1$ and that

$$T(n) = 3^{i-1}T(n - i + 1) + 2\sum_{j=0}^{i-2} 3^j.$$

Then,

$$
\begin{aligned}
T(n) &= 3^{i-1}T(n - i + 1) + 2\sum_{j=0}^{i-2} 3^j \\
&= 3^{i-1}(3T(n - i) + 2) + 2\sum_{j=0}^{i-2} 3^j \\
&= 3^i T(n - i) + 2\sum_{j=0}^{i-1} 3^j,
\end{aligned}
$$

as required. Now that we've established identity (4.1), we can continue with solving the recurrence. Suppose we take $i = n - 1$. Then, by identity (4.1),

$$
\begin{aligned}
T(n) &= 3^{n-1}T(1) + 2\sum_{j=0}^{n-2} 3^j \\
&= 3^{n-1} + 3^{n-1} - 1 \quad \text{(by Problem 9)} \\
&= 2 \cdot 3^{n-1} - 1.
\end{aligned}
$$

208. Suppose $T(1) = 1$, and for all $n \geq 2$ a power of 2, $T(n) = 2T(n/2) + 6n - 1$. If n is large enough, then by repeated substitution,

$$
\begin{aligned}
T(n) &= 2T(n/2) + 6n - 1 \quad \text{(after one substitution)} \\
&= 2(2T(n/4) + 6n/2 - 1) + 6n - 1 \\
&= 4T(n/4) + (6n - 2) + (6n - 1) \quad \text{(after two substitutions)} \\
&= 4(2T(n/8) + 6n/4 - 1) + (6n - 2) + (6n - 1) \\
&= 8T(n/8) + (6n - 4) + (6n - 2) + (6n - 1) \\
&\quad \text{(after three substitutions)}.
\end{aligned}
$$

Therefore, after i substitutions,

$$T(n) = 2^i T(n/2^i) + 6in - \sum_{j=0}^{i-1} 2^j.$$

This can be verified easily by induction. Hence, taking $i = \log n$,

$$
\begin{aligned}
T(n) &= nT(1) + 6n \log n - \sum_{j=0}^{\log n-1} 2^j \\
&= n + 6n \log n - (2^{\log n} - 1) \quad \text{(by Problem 11)} \\
&= 6n \log n + 1.
\end{aligned}
$$

214. Suppose $T(1) = 1$, and for all $n \geq 2$ a power of 2, $T(n) = 3T(n/2) + n^2 - n$. If n is large enough, then by repeated substitution,

$$
\begin{aligned}
T(n) &= 3T(n/2) + n^2 - n \quad \text{(after one substitution)} \\
&= 3(3T(n/4) + n^2/4 - n/2) + n^2 - n \\
&= 9T(n/4) + 3(n^2/4 - n/2) + (n^2 - n) \quad \text{(after two substitutions)} \\
&= 9(3T(n/8) + n^2/16 - n/4) + 3(n^2/4 - n/2) + (n^2 - n) \\
&= 27T(n/8) + 9(n^2/16 - n/4) + 3(n^2/4 - n/2) + (n^2 - n)
\end{aligned}
$$

(after three substitutions).

Therefore, after i substitutions,

$$
\begin{aligned}
T(n) &= 3^i T(n/2^i) + n^2 \sum_{j=0}^{i-1} (3/4)^j - n \sum_{j=0}^{i-1} (3/2)^j \\
&= 3^i T(n/2^i) - 4n^2(3/4)^i + 4n^2 - 2n(3/2)^i + 2n \quad \text{(by Problem 11)}.
\end{aligned}
$$

This can be verified easily by induction. Hence, taking $i = \log n$,

$$
\begin{aligned}
T(n) &= 3^{\log n} - 4n^2(3/4)^{\log n} + 4n^2 - 2n(3/2)^{\log n} + 2n \\
&= n^{\log 3} - 4n^{\log 3} + 4n^2 - 2n^{\log 3} + 2n \\
&= 4n^2 - 5n^{\log 3} + 2n.
\end{aligned}
$$

226. Suppose $T(1) = 1$, $T(2) = 6$, and for all $n \geq 3$, $T(n) = T(n-2) + 3n + 4$. If n is large enough, then by repeated substitution,

$$
\begin{aligned}
T(n) &= T(n-2) + 3n + 4 \\
&= T(n-4) + (3(n-2) + 4) + (3n + 4) \\
&= T(n-6) + (3(n-4) + 4) + (3(n-2) + 4) + (3n + 4).
\end{aligned}
$$

Therefore, after i substitutions,

$$
T(n) = T(n - 2i) + 3 \sum_{j=0}^{i-1} (n - 2j) + 4i
$$

$$= T(n - 2i) + 3in - 6 \sum_{j=0}^{i-1} j + 4i$$

$$= T(n - 2i) + 3in - 3i(i - 1) + 4i \quad \text{(by Problem 1)}$$

$$= T(n - 2i) + 3in - 3i^2 + 7i.$$

This can be verified easily by induction. Now, suppose that n is even. Take $i = n/2 - 1$. Then,

$$
\begin{aligned}
T(n) &= T(n - 2i) + 3in - 3i^2 + 7i \\
&= T(2) + 3(n/2 - 1)n - 3(n/2 - 1)^2 + 7(n/2 - 1) \\
&= 6 + 3n^2/2 - 3n - 3n^2/4 + 3n - 3 + 7n/2 - 7 \\
&= 3n^2/4 + 7n/2 - 4.
\end{aligned}
$$

Now, suppose that n is odd. Take $i = (n - 1)/2$. Then,

$$
\begin{aligned}
T(n) &= T(n - 2i) + 3 \sum_{j=0}^{i-1}(n - 2j) + 4i \\
&= T(1) + 3n(n - 1)/2 - 3((n - 1)/2)^2 + 7(n - 1)/2 \\
&= 1 + 3n^2/2 - 3n/2 - 3n^2/4 + 3n/2 - 3/4 + 7n/2 - 7/2 \\
&= 3n^2/4 + 7n/2 - 13/4.
\end{aligned}
$$

Therefore, when n is even, $T(n) = (3n^2 + 14n - 16)/4$, and when n is odd, $T(n) = (3n^2 + 14n - 13)/4$. Or, more succinctly, $T(n) = (3n^2 + 14n - 16 + 3(n \bmod 2))/4$.

235. Suppose that $T(1) = 1$, and for all $n \geq 2$, $T(n) = \sum_{i=1}^{n-1} T(i) + 1$.

$$
\begin{aligned}
T(n) - T(n - 1) &= (\sum_{i=1}^{n-1} T(i) + 1) - (\sum_{i=1}^{n-2} T(i) + 1) \\
&= T(n - 1).
\end{aligned}
$$

Therefore, $T(n) = 2T(n - 1)$. Thus, we have reduced a recurrence with full history to a simple recurrence that can be solved by repeated substitution (I'll leave that to you) to give the solution $T(n) = 2^{n-1}$.

4.8   COMMENTS

202. The technique used to solve this problem in the previous section is called *repeated substitution*. It works as follows. Repeatedly substitute until you see a pattern developing. Write down a formula for $T(n)$ in terms of n and the number of substitutions (which you can call i). To be completely formal,

verify this pattern by induction on i. (You should do this if you are asked to prove that your answer is correct or if you want to be sure that the pattern is right, but you can skip it is you are short of time.) Then choose i to be whatever value it takes to make all of the $T(\cdot)$s in the pattern turn into the base case for the recurrence. You are usually left with some algebra to do, such as a summation or two. Once you have used repeated substitution to get an answer, it is prudent to check your answer by using induction. (It is not normally necessary to hand in this extra work when you are asked to solve the recurrence on a homework or an exam, but it's a good idea to do it for your own peace of mind.) Let's do it for this problem. We are required to prove that the solution to the recurrence $T(1) = 1$, and for all $n \geq 2$, $T(n) = 3T(n-1) + 2$, is $T(n) = 2 \cdot 3^{n-1} - 1$. The proof is by induction on n. The claim is certainly true for $n = 1$. Now suppose that $n > 1$ and $T(n-1) = 2 \cdot 3^{n-2} - 1$. Then,

$$
\begin{aligned}
T(n) &= 3T(n-1) + 2 \\
&= 3(2 \cdot 3^{n-2} - 1) + 2 \quad \text{(by the induction hypothesis)} \\
&= 2 \cdot 3^{n-1} - 1,
\end{aligned}
$$

as required.

222. Hence, $F_n = O(1.62^n)$. For more information on the constant multiple in the big-O bound, see Graham, Knuth, and Patashnik [30].

Chapter 5

Correctness Proofs

How do we know that a given algorithm works? The best method is to prove it correct. Purely recursive algorithms can be proved correct directly by induction. Purely iterative algorithms can be proved correct by devising a *loop invariant* for every loop, proving them correct by induction, and using them to establish that the algorithm terminates with the correct result. Here are some simple algorithms to practice on. The algorithms use a simple pseudocode as described in Section 1.3.

5.1   ITERATIVE ALGORITHMS

To prove correctness of an iterative algorithm, you need to do the following:

- Write down a specification for the output to be produced by the algorithm as a function of its inputs (this will be easy for the simple algorithms considered in this chapter).
- Verify the algorithm one loop at a time, starting at the inner loop in case of nested loops.
- For each loop, devise a *loop invariant* that remains true each time through the loop and captures the "progress" made by the loop.
- Prove that the loop invariants hold. This is usually done by induction on the number of iterations. Start by listing the new values of the variables in terms of the old values. Use this for your inductive step.
- Use the loop invariants to prove that the algorithm terminates.
- Use the loop invariants and the termination conditions to prove that the algorithm computes the correct result (according to the specification).

The loop invariants discussed in this section use the following convention: If v is a variable used in a loop, then v_j denotes the value stored in v immediately after the jth iteration of the loop, for $j \geq 0$. The value v_0 means the contents of v immediately before the loop is entered.

46

5.1.1 Straight-Line Programs

249. ☞ Prove that the following algorithm for swapping two numbers is correct.

procedure swap(x, y)
comment Swap x and y.

1.	$x := x + y$
2.	$y := x - y$
3.	$x := x - y$

5.1.2 Arithmetic

250. ☞ ☼ 🖙 Prove that the following algorithm for the addition of natural numbers is correct.

function add(y, z)
comment Return $y + z$, where $y, z \in \mathbb{N}$

1.	$x := 0;\ c := 0;\ d := 1;$
2.	**while** $(y > 0) \vee (z > 0) \vee (c > 0)$ **do**
3.	$\quad a := y \bmod 2;$
	$\quad b := z \bmod 2;$
4.	$\quad$ **if** $a \oplus b \oplus c$ **then** $x := x + d;$
5.	$\quad c := (a \wedge b) \vee (b \wedge c) \vee (a \wedge c);$
6.	$\quad d := 2d;\ y := \lfloor y/2 \rfloor;$
	$\quad z := \lfloor z/2 \rfloor;$
7.	**return**(x)

251. ☞ Prove that the following algorithm for incrementing a natural number is correct.

function increment(y)
comment Return $y + 1$, where $y \in \mathbb{N}$

1.	$x := 0;\ c := 1;\ d := 1;$
2.	**while** $(y > 0) \vee (c > 0)$ **do**
3.	$\quad a := y \bmod 2;$
4.	$\quad$ **if** $a \oplus c$ **then** $x := x + d;$
5.	$\quad c := a \wedge c;$
6.	$\quad d := 2d;\ y := \lfloor y/2 \rfloor;$
7.	**return**(x)

252. ☞ ☼ Prove that the following algorithm for the multiplication of natural numbers is correct.

```
              function multiply(y, z)
                 comment Return yz, where y, z ∈ N
1.               x := 0;
2.               while z > 0 do
3.                  if z mod 2 = 1 then x := x + y;
4.                  y := 2y; z := ⌊z/2⌋;
5.               return(x)
```

253. ☞☞☺☞ Prove that the following algorithm for the multiplication of natural numbers is correct.

```
              function multiply(y, z)
                 comment Return yz, where y, z ∈ N
1.               x := 0;
2.               while z > 0 do
3.                  x := x + y · (z mod 2);
4.                  y := 2y; z := ⌊z/2⌋;
5.               return(x)
```

254. ☞☞ Prove that the following algorithm for the multiplication of natural numbers is correct, for all integer constants $c \geq 2$.

```
              function multiply(y, z)
                 comment Return yz, where y, z ∈ N
1.               x := 0;
2.               while z > 0 do
3.                  x := x + y · (z mod c);
4.                  y := c · y; z := ⌊z/c⌋;
5.               return(x)
```

255. ☞ ※ Prove that the following algorithm for division and remaindering of natural numbers is correct.

```
              function divide(y, z)
                 comment Return q, r ∈ N such that y = qz + r
                 and r < z, where y, z ∈ N
1.               r := y; q := 0; w := z;
2.               while w ≤ y do w := 2w;
3.               while w > z do
4.                  q := 2q; w := ⌊w/2⌋;
5.                  if w ≤ r then
6.                     r := r − w; q := q + 1
7.               return(q, r)
```

256. ☞ ☼ Prove that the following algorithm for exponentiation is correct.

> **function** power(y, z)
>   **comment** Return y^z, where $y \in \mathbb{R}$, $z \in \mathbb{N}$
> 1. $x := 1$;
> 2.   **while** $z > 0$ **do**
> 3. $x := x \cdot y$
> 4. $z := z - 1$
> 5.   **return**(x)

257. ☞ ☼ Prove that the following algorithm for exponentiation is correct.

> **function** power(y, z)
>   **comment** Return y^z, where $y \in \mathbb{R}$, $z \in \mathbb{N}$
> 1. $x := 1$;
> 2.   **while** $z > 0$ **do**
> 3.   **if** z is odd **then** $x := x \cdot y$
> 4. $z := \lfloor z/2 \rfloor$
> 5. $y := y^2$
> 6.   **return**(x)

258. ☞ ☼ Prove that the following algorithm for computing factorials is correct.

> **function** factorial(y)
>   **comment** Return $y!$, where $y \in \mathbb{N}$
> 1. $x := 1$
> 2.   **while** $y > 1$ **do**
> 3. $x := x \cdot y$; $y := y - 1$
> 4.   **return**(x)

5.1.3 Arrays

259. ☞ ☼ Prove that the following algorithm that adds the values in an array $A[1..n]$ is correct.

> **function** sum(A)
>   **comment** Return $\sum_{i=1}^{n} A[i]$
> 1. $s := 0$;
> 2.   **for** $i := 1$ **to** n **do**
> 3. $s := s + A[i]$
> 4.   **return**(s)

260. ☞ ☼ Prove that the following algorithm for computing the maximum value in an array $A[1..n]$ is correct.

>**function** max(A)
> **comment** Return max $A[1], \ldots, A[n]$
>1. $m := A[1]$
>2. **for** $i := 2$ **to** n **do**
>3.   **if** $A[i] > m$ **then** $m := A[i]$
>4. **return**(m)

261. ☞☞ ☼ Prove the correctness of the following bubblesort algorithm. The values to be sorted are in an array $A[1..n]$.

>**procedure** bubblesort($A[1..n]$)
> **comment** Sort $A[1], A[2], \ldots, A[n]$ into nondecreasing order
>1. **for** $i := 1$ **to** $n-1$ **do**
>2.   **for** $j := 1$ **to** $n-i$ **do**
>3.   **if** $A[j] > A[j+1]$ **then**
>4.   Swap $A[j]$ with $A[j+1]$

262. ☞☞ Prove the correctness of the following pattern-matching algorithm. The input consists of a string $S[1..n]$, and a pattern $P[0..m-1]$, where $1 \leq m \leq n$. The algorithm locates the first contiguous occurrence of the pattern P in the string S, that is, $\ell = p$ if $S[p..p+m-1] = P$, and $\ell = n-m+1$ if the pattern P does not occur at all in the string S.

>**function** match(P, S, n, m)
> **comment** Find the pattern $P[0..m-1]$ in string $S[1..n]$
>1. $\ell := 0$; matched := **false**
>2. **while** $(\ell \leq n-m) \wedge \neg$matched **do**
>3. $\ell := \ell + 1$;
>4. $r := 0$; matched := **true**
>5.   **while** $(r < m) \wedge$ matched **do**
>6.   matched := matched $\wedge$ $(P[r] = S[\ell+r])$
>7. $r := r + 1$
>8. **return**(ℓ)

263. ☞☞ Prove that the following matrix multiplication algorithm is correct.

$$\textbf{procedure } \text{matmultiply}(Y, Z, n);$$
$$\textbf{comment } \text{multiplies } n \times n \text{ matrices } YZ$$

1.   **for** $i := 1$ **to** n **do**
2.   **for** $j := 1$ **to** n **do**
3. $X[i,j] := 0;$
4.   **for** $k := 1$ **to** n **do**
5. $X[i,j] := X[i,j] + Y[i,k] \cdot Z[k,j];$
6.   **return**(X)

264. Prove that the following algorithm for evaluating the polynomial $a_n x^n + a_{n-1} x^{n-1} + \cdots + a_1 x + a_0$ is correct, where the coefficients are stored in an array $A[0..n]$, with $A[i] = a_i$ for all $0 \le i \le n$. The algorithm is named after its inventor, William G. Horner, and is often called *Horner's rule*.

$$\textbf{function } \text{Horner}(A, n)$$
$$\textbf{comment } \text{Return } \sum_{i=0}^{n} A[i] \cdot x^i$$

1. $v := 0$
2.   **for** $i := n$ **downto** 0 **do**
3. $v := A[i] + v \cdot x$
4.   **return**(v)

5.1.4 Fibonacci Numbers

265. Prove that the following algorithm for computing Fibonacci numbers is correct.

$$\textbf{function } \text{fib}(n)$$

1.   **comment** Return F_n, the nth Fibonacci number
2.   **if** $n = 0$ **then return**(0) **else**
3.   last:=0; current:=1
4.   **for** $i := 2$ **to** n **do**
5.   temp:=last+current; last:=current; current:=temp
6.   **return**(current)

5.2 RECURSIVE ALGORITHMS

To prove correctness of a recursive algorithm, you need to do the following:

- You will prove correctness by induction on the "size" of the problem being solved (for example, the size of array chunk, number of bits in an integer, etc.). Your first task is to identify what is to be used as the "size."

- Then, you prove the base of the induction, which will usually involve only the base of the recursion.
- Next, you need to prove that recursive calls are given subproblems to solve (that is, there is no infinite recursion). This is often trivial, but it can be difficult to prove and so should not be overlooked.
- Finally, you prove the inductive step: Assume that the recursive calls work correctly, and use this assumption to prove that the current call works correctly.

5.2.1 Arithmetic

266. ☞ Prove that the following recursive algorithm computes $3^n - 2^n$ for all $n \geq 0$.

$$\begin{aligned}
&\textbf{function } g(n)\\
1.\quad &\quad \textbf{if } n \leq 1 \textbf{ then return}(n)\\
2.\quad &\quad \textbf{else return}(5 \cdot g(n-1) - 6 \cdot g(n-2))
\end{aligned}$$

267. ☞ Prove that the following recursive algorithm for incrementing a natural number is correct.

$$\begin{aligned}
&\textbf{function } \text{increment}(y)\\
&\quad \textbf{comment } \text{Return } y + 1.\\
1.\quad &\quad \textbf{if } y = 0 \textbf{ then return}(1) \textbf{ else}\\
2.\quad &\quad\quad \textbf{if } y \bmod 2 = 1 \textbf{ then}\\
3.\quad &\quad\quad\quad \text{return}(2 \cdot \text{increment}(\lfloor y/2 \rfloor))\\
4.\quad &\quad\quad \textbf{else return}(y + 1)
\end{aligned}$$

268. ☞ Prove that the following recursive algorithm for the addition of natural numbers is correct.

$$\begin{aligned}
&\textbf{function } \text{add}(y, z, c)\\
&\quad \textbf{comment } \text{Return the sum } y + z + c, \text{ where } c \in \{0, 1\}.\\
1.\quad &\quad \textbf{if } y = z = 0 \textbf{ then return}(c) \textbf{ else}\\
2.\quad &\quad a := y \bmod 2; \ b := z \bmod 2;\\
3.\quad &\quad \text{return}(2 \cdot \text{add}(\lfloor y/2 \rfloor, \lfloor z/2 \rfloor, \lfloor (a+b+c)/2 \rfloor) + (a \oplus b \oplus c))
\end{aligned}$$

269. ☞ 🖎 Prove that the following recursive algorithm for the multiplication of natural numbers is correct.

$$\begin{aligned}
&\textbf{function } \text{multiply}(y, z)\\
&\quad \textbf{comment } \text{Return the product } yz.\\
1.\quad &\quad \textbf{if } z = 0 \textbf{ then return}(0) \textbf{ else}\\
2.\quad &\quad \textbf{if } z \text{ is odd } \textbf{then } \text{return}(\text{multiply}(2y, \lfloor z/2 \rfloor)+y)\\
3.\quad &\quad \textbf{else return}(\text{multiply}(2y, \lfloor z/2 \rfloor))
\end{aligned}$$

270. ☞ Prove that the following recursive algorithm for the multiplication of natural numbers is correct.

> **function** multiply(y, z)
>   **comment** Return the product yz.
> 1.   **if** $z = 0$ **then** return(0) **else**
> 2.   return(multiply$(2y, \lfloor z/2 \rfloor) + y \cdot (z \bmod 2))$

271. ☞ Prove that the following recursive algorithm for the multiplication of natural numbers is correct, for all integers constants $c \geq 2$.

> **function** multiply(y, z)
>   **comment** Return the product yz.
> 1.   **if** $z = 0$ **then** return(0) **else**
> 2.   return(multiply$(cy, \lfloor z/c \rfloor) + y \cdot (z \bmod c))$

272. ☞ Prove that the following recursive algorithm for exponentiation is correct.

> **function** power(y, z)
>   **comment** Return y^z, where $y \in \mathbf{R}$, $z \in \mathbf{N}$.
> 1.   **if** $z = 0$ **then** return(1)
> 2.   **if** z is odd **then** return(power$(y^2, \lfloor z/2 \rfloor) \cdot y)$
> 3.   **else** return(power$(y^2, \lfloor z/2 \rfloor))$

273. ☞ Prove that the following recursive algorithm for computing factorials is correct.

> **function** factorial(n)
>   **comment** Return $n!$.
> 1.   **if** $n \leq 1$ **then** return(1)
> 2.   **else** return$(n \cdot$ factorial$(n - 1))$

5.2.2 Arrays

274. ☞ Prove that the following recursive algorithm for computing the maximum value in an array $A[1..n]$ is correct.

> **function** maximum(n)
>   **comment** Return max of $A[1..n]$.
> 1.   **if** $n \leq 1$ **then** return$(A[1])$
> 2.   **else** return(max(maximum$(n - 1), A[n]))$

> **function** max(x, y)
>   **comment** Return largest of x and y.
> 3.   **if** $x \geq y$ **then** return(x) **else** return(y)

275. ☞ Prove that the following recursive algorithm that adds the values in an array $A[1..n]$ is correct.

> **function** sum(n)
>   **comment** Return sum of $A[1..n]$.
> 1.   **if** $n \leq 1$ **then** return($A[1]$)
> 2.   **else** return(sum($n-1$) + $A[n]$)

5.2.3 Fibonacci Numbers

276. ☞ ☺☞ Prove that the following algorithm for computing Fibonacci numbers is correct.

> **function** fib(n)
>   **comment** Return F_n, the nth Fibonacci number.
> 1.   **if** $n \leq 1$ **then** return(n)
> 2.   **else** return(fib($n-1$)+fib($n-2$))

277. ☞☞ ☀ ☺☞ Prove that the following algorithm for computing Fibonacci numbers is correct.

> **function** fib(n)
>   **comment** Return (F_{n-1}, F_n)
> 1.   **if** n is odd **then**
> 2. $(a,b) := $ even($n-1$)
> 3.   **return**($b, a+b$)
> 4.   **else return**(even(n))
>
> **function** even(n)
>   **comment** Return (F_{n-1}, F_n) when n is even
> 1.   **if** $n = 0$ **then return**($1, 0$)
> 2.   **else if** $n = 2$ **then return**($1, 1$)
> 3.   **else if** $n = 4$ **then return**($2, 3$)
> 4. $(a,b) := $ fib($n/2 - 1$)
> 5. $c := a + b; d := b + c$
> 6.   **return**($b \cdot d + a \cdot c, c \cdot (d + b)$)

5.3 COMBINED ITERATION AND RECURSION

The following questions ask you to prove correct some recursive algorithms that have loops in them. Naturally enough, you can solve them by applying both of the techniques you have used in this chapter.

278. ☞ Prove that the following recursive bubblesort algorithm is correct. The values to be sorted are in an array $A[1..n]$.

procedure bubblesort(n)
    comment Sort $A[1..n]$.

1.   **if** $n > 1$ **then**
2.   **for** $j := 1$ **to** $n - 1$ **do**
3.   **if** $A[j] > A[j + 1]$ **then**
4.   Swap $A[j]$ with $A[j + 1]$
5.   bubblesort($n - 1$)

279. ☞ ☞ Prove that the following variant of quicksort is correct. The values to be sorted are in an array $A[1..n]$.

1.   **procedure** quicksort(ℓ, r)
2.   **comment** sort $S[\ell..r]$
3. $i := \ell; j := r$
           $a :=$ some element from $S[\ell..r]$
4.   **repeat**
5.   **while** $S[i] < a$ **do** $i := i + 1$
6.   **while** $S[j] > a$ **do** $j := j - 1$
7.   **if** $i \leq j$ **then**
8.   swap $S[i]$ and $S[j]$
9. $i := i + 1; j := j - 1$
10.   **until** $i > j$
11.   **if** $\ell < j$ **then** quicksort(ℓ, j)
12.   **if** $i < r$ **then** quicksort(i, r)

5.4 HINTS

In each of the following hints, if the algorithm uses a variable v, then v_i denotes the contents of v immediately after the ith iteration of the single loop in the algorithm (v_0 denotes the contents of v immediately before the loop is entered for the first time).

250. The loop invariant is the following: $(y_j + z_j + c_j)d_j + x_j = y_0 + z_0$.

252. The loop invariant is the following: $y_j z_j + x_j = y_0 z_0$.

255. The loop invariant is the following: $q_j w_j + r_j = y_0$ and $r_j < w_j$.

256. The loop invariant is the following: $x_j y_j{}^{z_j} = y_0^{z_0}$.

257. The loop invariant is the following: $x_j y_j{}^{z_j} = y_0{}^{z_0}$.

258. The loop invariant is the following: $m_j = \prod_{k=n-j+1}^{n} k$.

259. The loop invariant is the following: $s_j = \sum_{i=1}^{j} A[i]$.

260. The loop invariant is the following: m_j is the maximum of $A[1], \ldots, A[j+1]$.

261. The loop invariant for the inner loop is the following: after the jth iteration, for all $1 \le i < j$, $A[i] \le A[j]$. The loop invariant for the outer loop is the following: after the jth iteration, for all $n - j + 1 \le i \le n$, for all $k < i$, $A[k] \le A[i]$.

277. The identity from Problem 53 might help.

5.5 SOLUTIONS

250. This correctness proof will make use of the fact that for all $n \in \mathbb{N}$,

$$2\lfloor n/2 \rfloor + (n \bmod 2) = n. \tag{5.1}$$

(Can you prove this?) We claim that if $y, z \in \mathbb{N}$, then add(y, z) returns the value $y + z$. That is, when line 8 is executed, $x = y + z$. For each of the identifiers, use a subscript i to denote the value of the identifier after the ith iteration of the while-loop on lines 3–7, for $i \ge 0$, with $i = 0$ meaning the time immediately before the while loop is entered and immediately after the statement on line 2 is executed. By inspection,

$$
\begin{aligned}
a_{j+1} &= y_j \bmod 2 \\
b_{j+1} &= z_j \bmod 2 \\
y_{j+1} &= \lfloor y_j/2 \rfloor \\
z_{j+1} &= \lfloor z_j/2 \rfloor \\
d_{j+1} &= 2d_j.
\end{aligned}
$$

From line 6 of the algorithm, c_{j+1} is 1 iff at least two of a_{j+1}, b_{j+1}, and c_j are 1 (see Problem 93). Therefore,

$$c_{j+1} = \lfloor (a_{j+1} + b_{j+1} + c_j)/2 \rfloor.$$

Note that d is added into x in line 5 of the algorithm only when an odd number of a, b, and c are 1. Therefore,

$$x_{j+1} = x_j + d_j((a_{j+1} + b_{j+1} + c_j) \bmod 2).$$

We will now prove the following loop invariant: For all natural numbers $j \ge 0$,

$$(y_j + z_j + c_j)d_j + x_j = y_0 + z_0.$$

The proof is by induction on j. The base $j = 0$ is trivial, since $c_0 = 0$, $d_0 = 1$, and $x_0 = 0$. Now, suppose that

$$(y_j + z_j + c_j)d_j + x_j = y_0 + z_0.$$

We are required to prove that

$$(y_{j+1} + z_{j+1} + c_{j+1})d_{j+1} + x_{j+1} = y_0 + z_0.$$

By the preceding,

$$
\begin{aligned}
&(y_{j+1} + z_{j+1} + c_{j+1})d_{j+1} + x_{j+1} \\
={} &(\lfloor y_j/2 \rfloor + \lfloor z_j/2 \rfloor + \lfloor (y_j \bmod 2 + z_j \bmod 2 + c_j)/2 \rfloor)2d_j \\
&+ x_j + d_j((y_j \bmod 2 + z_j \bmod 2 + c_j) \bmod 2) \\
={} &(\lfloor y_j/2 \rfloor + \lfloor z_j/2 \rfloor)2d_j + x_j + d_j(y_j \bmod 2 + z_j \bmod 2 + c_j) \\
&\text{(by Equation 5.1)} \\
={} &(y_j + z_j + c_j)d_j + x_j \quad \text{(by Equation 5.1 twice).}
\end{aligned}
$$

Therefore, by the induction hypothesis,

$$(y_{j+1} + z_{j+1} + c_{j+1})d_{j+1} + x_{j+1} = y_0 + z_0.$$

This ends the proof of the loop invariant. It remains to use it to prove that the algorithm is correct. We need to prove that the algorithm terminates with x containing the sum of y and z. First, we will prove that it terminates. By inspection, the values of y and z are halved (rounding down if they are odd) on every iteration of the loop. Therefore, they will eventually both have value zero, and stay that way. At the first point at which $y = z = 0$, either c will equal zero or c will be assigned zero on the next iteration of the loop. Therefore, eventually $y = z = c = 0$, at which point the loop terminates. Now we will prove that x has the correct value on termination. Suppose the loop terminates after t iterations, for some $t \geq 0$. By the loop invariant,

$$(y_t + z_t + c_t)d_t + x_t = y_0 + z_0.$$

Since $y_t = z_t = c_t = 0$, we see that $x_t = y_0 + z_0$. Therefore, the algorithm terminates with x containing the sum of the initial values of y and z, as required.

269. The correctness proof is by induction on z. We claim that $\text{multiply}(y, z)$ returns the product yz. The hypothesis is true for $z = 0$, since $\text{multiply}(y, 0)$ returns 0. Now, suppose that for $z \geq 0$, $\text{multiply}(y, z)$ returns yz. We now must prove that $\text{multiply}(y, z + 1)$ returns $y(z + 1)$. There are two cases to be considered, depending on whether $z + 1$ is odd or even. By inspection, if

$z + 1$ is odd, then multiply$(y, z + 1)$ returns

$$
\begin{aligned}
& \text{multiply}(2y, \lfloor (z+1)/2 \rfloor) + y \\
=\ & 2y\lfloor (z+1)/2 \rfloor + y \quad \text{(by the induction hypothesis)} \\
=\ & 2y(z/2) + y \quad \text{(since } z \text{ is even)} \\
=\ & y(z+1).
\end{aligned}
$$

By inspection, if $z + 1$ is even, then multiply$(y, z + 1)$ returns

$$
\begin{aligned}
& \text{multiply}(2y, \lfloor (z+1)/2 \rfloor) \\
=\ & 2y\lfloor (z+1)/2 \rfloor \quad \text{(by the induction hypothesis)} \\
=\ & 2y(z+1)/2 \quad \text{(since } z \text{ is odd)} \\
=\ & y(z+1).
\end{aligned}
$$

5.6   COMMENTS

253. The hard part about this problem (and other similar problems in this section) is that you will need to find your own loop invariant.

265. See Section 2.7 for the definition of Fibonacci numbers. This is the obvious iterative algorithm.

276. See Section 2.7 for the definition of Fibonacci numbers. This is the obvious recursive algorithm.

277. See Section 2.7 for the definition of Fibonacci numbers. This is a sneaky recursive algorithm.

Chapter 6

Algorithm Analysis

Algorithm analysis usually means "give a big-O figure for the running time of an algorithm." (Of course, a big-Θ bound would be even better.) This can be done by getting a big-O figure for parts of the algorithm and then combining these figures using the sum and product rules for big-O (see Problems 173 and 176). As we will see, recursive algorithms are more difficult to analyze than nonrecursive ones.

Another useful technique is to pick an elementary operation, such as additions, multiplications, or comparisons, and observe that the running time of the algorithm is big-O of the number of elementary operations. (To find the elementary operation, just ignore the "book keeping" code and look for the point in the algorithm where the real work is done.) Then, you can analyze the exact number of elementary operations as a function of n in the worst case. This is often easier to deal with because it is an exact function of n and you don't have the messy big-O symbols to carry through your analysis.

6.1 ITERATIVE ALGORITHMS

The analysis of iterative algorithms is fairly easy. Simply charge $O(1)$ for code without loops (assuming that your pseudocode isn't hiding something that takes longer), and use the sum and product rules for big-O (see Problems 173 and 176). If you get tired of carrying around big-Os, use the "elementary operation" technique described earlier.

6.1.1 What is Returned?

280. ☞ ☞ What is the value returned by the following function? Express your answer as a function of n. Give, using big-O notation, the worst-case running time.

function mystery(n)
1. $r := 0$;
2.   **for** $i := 1$ **to** $n - 1$ **do**
3.   **for** $j := i + 1$ **to** n **do**
4.   **for** $k := 1$ **to** j **do**
5. $r := r + 1$
6.   return(r)

281. ☞ What is the value returned by the following function? Express your answer as a function of n. Give, using big-O notation, the worst-case running time.

function pesky(n)
1. $r := 0$;
2.   **for** $i := 1$ **to** n **do**
3.   **for** $j := 1$ **to** i **do**
4.   **for** $k := j$ **to** $i + j$ **do**
5. $r := r + 1$
6.   return(r)

282. ☞☞ What is the value returned by the following function? Express your answer as a function of n. Give, using big-O notation, the worst-case running time.

function pestiferous(n)
1. $r := 0$;
2.   **for** $i := 1$ **to** n **do**
3.   **for** $j := 1$ **to** i **do**
4.   **for** $k := j$ **to** $i + j$ **do**
5.   **for** $\ell := 1$ **to** $i + j - k$ **do**
6. $r := r + 1$
7.   return(r)

283. ☞☞☞ ☀ What is the value returned by the following function? Express your answer as a function of n. Give, using big-O notation, the worst-case running time.

function conundrum(n)
1. $r := 0$;
2.   **for** $i := 1$ **to** n **do**
3.   **for** $j := i + 1$ **to** n **do**
4.   **for** $k := i + j - 1$ **to** n **do**
5. $r := r + 1$
6.   return(r)

6.1.2 Arithmetic

284. ☞ ⚗ Analyze the algorithm for the addition of natural numbers in Problem 250. How many additions does it use (that is, how many times is line 4 executed) in the worst case?

285. ☞ Analyze the algorithm for incrementing a natural number in Problem 251. How many additions does it use (that is, how many times is line 4 executed) in the worst case?

286. ☞ Analyze the algorithm for the multiplication of natural numbers in Problem 252. How many additions does it use (that is, how many times is line 3 executed) in the worst case?

287. ☞ Analyze the algorithm for the multiplication of natural numbers in Problem 253. How many additions does it use (that is, how many times is line 3 executed) in the worst case?

288. ☞ Analyze the algorithm for the multiplication of natural numbers in Problem 254. How many additions does it use (that is, how many times is line 3 executed) in the worst case? You may assume that $c \geq 2$ is an integer.

289. ☞ Analyze the algorithm for division and remaindering of natural numbers in Problem 255. How many subtractions does it use (that is, how many times is line 6 executed) in the worst case?

290. ☞ Analyze the algorithm for exponentiation in Problem 256. How many multiplications does it use (that is, how many times is line 3 executed) in the worst case?

291. ☞ ☺↶ Analyze the algorithm for exponentiation in Problem 257. How many multiplications does it use (that is, how many times is line 3 executed) in the worst case?

292. ☞ Analyze the algorithm for computing factorials in Problem 258. How many multiplications does it use (that is, how many times is line 3 executed) in the worst case?

6.1.3 Arrays

293. ☞ Analyze the array addition algorithm in Problem 259. How many additions does it use (that is, how many times is line 3 executed) in the worst case?

294. ☞ Analyze the array maximum algorithm in Problem 260. How many comparisons does it use (that is, how many times is line 3 executed) in the worst case?

295. ☞ Analyze the bubblesort algorithm in Problem 261. How many comparisons does it use (that is, how many times is line 3 executed) in the worst case?

296. ☞ Analyze the pattern-matching algorithm in Problem 262. How many accesses of the array P does it use (that is, how many times is line 6 executed) in the worst case?

297. ☞ Analyze the matrix multiplication algorithm in Problem 263. How many multiplications does it use (that is, how many times is line 5 executed) in the worst case?

298. ☞ Analyze the algorithm for evaluating a polynomial in Problem 264. How many multiplications does it use (that is, how many times is line 3 executed) in the worst case?

6.1.4 Fibonacci Numbers

299. ☞ Analyze the algorithm for computing Fibonacci numbers in Problem 265. How many additions does it use (that is, how many times is line 3 executed) in the worst case?

6.2 RECURSIVE ALGORITHMS

The analysis of recursive algorithms is a little harder than that of nonrecursive ones. First, you have to derive a recurrence relation for the running time, and then you have to solve it. Techniques for the solution of recurrence relations are explained in Chapter 4.

To derive a recurrence relation for the running time of an algorithm:

- Decide what "n", the problem size, is.
- See what value of n is used as the base of the recursion. It will usually be a single value (for example, $n = 1$), but may be multiple values. Suppose it is n_0.
- Figure out what $T(n_0)$ is. You can usually use "some constant c," but sometimes a specific number will be needed.
- The general $T(n)$ is usually a sum of various choices of $T(m)$ (for the recursive calls), plus the sum of the other work done. Usually, the recursive calls will be solving a subproblems of the same size $f(n)$, giving a term "$a \cdot T(f(n))$" in the recurrence relation.

The "elementary operation" technique described in the first paragraph of this chapter can be used to good effect here, too.

6.2.1 Arithmetic

300. ✑✑ 🎓 ☞ Analyze the recursive algorithm from Problem 266. How many additions does it use (that is, how many times is line 2 executed) in the worst case?

301. ✑ Analyze the recursive algorithm for incrementing a natural number in Problem 267. How many right-shifts does it use (that is, how many times is line 3 executed) in the worst case?

302. ✑ Analyze the recursive algorithm for the addition of natural numbers in Problem 268. How many times is line 3 executed in the worst case?

303. ✑ ☞ Analyze the recursive algorithm for the multiplication of natural numbers in Problem 269. How many additions does it use (that is, how many times is line 2 executed) in the worst case?

304. ✑ Analyze the recursive algorithm for the multiplication of natural numbers in Problem 270. How many additions does it use (that is, how many times is line 2 executed) in the worst case?

305. ✑ Analyze the recursive algorithm for the multiplication of natural numbers in Problem 271. How many additions does it use (that is, how many times is line 2 executed) in the worst case? You may assume that $c \geq 2$ is an integer.

306. ✑ Analyze the recursive algorithm for exponentiation in Problem 272. How many multiplications does it use (that is, how many times is line 2 executed) in the worst case?

307. ✑ Analyze the recursive algorithm for computing factorials in Problem 273. How many multiplications does it use (that is, how many times is line 2 executed) in the worst case?

6.2.2 Arrays

308. ✑ Analyze the recursive algorithm for computing the maximum value in an array in Problem 274. How many comparisons does it use (that is, how many times is line 2 executed) in the worst case?

309. ✑ Analyze the recursive algorithm that adds the values in an array in Problem 275. How many additions does it use (that is, how many times is line 2 executed) in the worst case?

6.2.3   Fibonacci Numbers

310. ☞ Analyze the algorithm for computing Fibonacci numbers in Problem 276. How many additions does it use (that is, how many times is line 2 executed) in the worst case?

311. ☞ ☺☞ Analyze the algorithm for computing Fibonacci numbers in Problem 277. How many additions does it use (that is, how many times is line 3 executed) in the worst case?

6.3   COMBINED ITERATION AND RECURSION

The following questions ask you to analyze some recursive algorithms that have loops in them. Naturally enough, you can do this by applying both of the techniques you have used in this chapter.

312. ☞ Analyze the recursive version of bubblesort in Problem 278. How many comparisons does it use (that is, how many times is line 3 executed) in the worst case?

313. ☞ ☺☞ Analyze the variant of quicksort in Problem 279. How many comparisons does it use (that is, how many times are lines 5 and 6 executed) in the worst case?

6.4   HINTS

283 If you use the technique from the solution of Problem 280 blindly, you'll get the answer $n(n-1)/2$. This is wrong. More subtlety is necessary. The correct answer is $n(n+2)(2n-1)/24$ if n is even, and something different if n is odd. (You didn't think I would give you the whole answer, did you?) You can partially verify your solution in a few minutes by coding the algorithm as a program and printing n and r for a few values of n.

284. I am looking for a big-O analysis of the running time, and an exact function of n (with no big-O at the front) for the number of additions. You can do the running time first, or if you are clever, you can observe that additions are the "elementary operation," count them exactly, and then put a big-O around the function you get as answer to the second part of the question (reducing it to the simplest form, of course) to give the answer for the first part of the question.

300. Fibonacci numbers are involved (see Section 2.7 for definitions). Specifically, you will need to apply the results from Problems 52 and 222.

6.5 SOLUTIONS

280. The for-loop on lines 4–5 has the same effect as $r := r + j$. Therefore, the for-loop on lines 3–5 has the following effect:

3–5.   **for** $j := i + 1$ **to** n **do**
$$r := r + j,$$

equivalently, $r := r + \sum_{j=i+1}^{n} j$. Now,

$$\sum_{j=i+1}^{n} j = \sum_{j=1}^{n} j - \sum_{j=1}^{i} j = n(n+1)/2 - i(i+1)/2.$$

Therefore, the for-loop on lines 2–5 has the following effect:

2–5.   **for** $i := 1$ **to** $n - 1$ **do**
$$r := r + n(n+1)/2 - i(i+1)/2,$$

equivalently, $r := r + \sum_{i=1}^{n-1}(n(n+1)/2 - i(i+1)/2)$. Now,

$$\sum_{i=1}^{n-1}(n(n+1)/2 - i(i+1)/2)$$

$$= \frac{(n-1)n(n+1)}{2} - \frac{1}{2}\sum_{i=1}^{n-1} i^2 - \frac{1}{2}\sum_{i=1}^{n-1} i$$

$$= (n-1)n(n+1)/2 - n(n-1)(2n-1)/12 - n(n-1)/4$$

(by Problems 1 and 2)

$$= n(n^2 - 1)/3.$$

Therefore, function mystery returns $n(n^2 - 1)/3$. A sloppy analysis goes as follows. The for-loop that begins on line 2 is executed for $O(n)$ iterations. The for-loop that begins on line 3 is executed for $O(n)$ iterations. The for-loop that begins on line 4 is executed for $O(n)$ iterations. Lines 1 and 5 take $O(1)$ time. Therefore, function mystery runs in time $O(n^3)$. This analysis is tight because the preceding paragraph showed that line 5 is executed $n(n^2 - 1)/3$ times.

300. Let $A(n)$ be the number of additions used in function $g(n)$. Then $A(0) = A(1) = 0$ and for all $n > 1$, $A(n) = A(n-1) + A(n-2) + 1$. This recurrence relation is a little tricky to solve, but repeated substitution will do it:

$$\begin{aligned} A(n) &= A(n-1) + A(n-2) + 1 \\ &= (A(n-2) + A(n-3) + 1) + A(n-2) + 1 \end{aligned}$$

$$
\begin{aligned}
&= & 2A(n-2) + A(n-3) + 1 + 1 \\
&= & 2(A(n-3) + A(n-4) + 1) + A(n-3) + 1 + 1 \\
&= & 3A(n-3) + 2A(n-4) + 1 + 1 + 2 \\
&= & 3(A(n-4) + A(n-5) + 1) + 2A(n-4) + 1 + 1 + 2 \\
&= & 5A(n-4) + 3A(n-5) + 1 + 1 + 2 + 3.
\end{aligned}
$$

There is a pattern involving Fibonacci numbers (see Section 2.7) developing here. It can be verified by induction on $i \geq 1$ that after i substitutions,

$$
A(n) = F_{i+1} A(n-i) + F_i A(n-i-1) + \sum_{j=1}^{i} F_j.
$$

Hence, taking $i = n - 1$,

$$
\begin{aligned}
A(n) &= & F_n A(1) + F_{n-1} A(0) + \sum_{j=1}^{n-1} F_j \\
&= & \sum_{j=1}^{n-1} F_j \\
&= & F_{n+1} - 1 \quad \text{(see Problem 52)}.
\end{aligned}
$$

The running time of procedure $g(n)$ is clearly big-O of the number of additions, and is hence $O(F_{n+1}) = O(1.62^n)$ (for the latter, see the comment to Problem 222).

303. Let n be the number of bits in z, and $A(n)$ be the number of additions used in the multiplication of y by z. Then $A(0) = 0$ and for all $n \geq 1$, $A(n) = A(n-1) + 1$. The solution to this recurrence is $A(n) = n$. (Can you verify this by induction on n? If I didn't tell you the answer, could you have derived it for yourself?) The running time of procedure multiply is clearly big-O of the number of additions, and is hence $O(n)$.

6.6   COMMENTS

291. Which algorithm would *you* use in practice, the one in this problem or the one from Problem 290?

311. Which algorithm would *you* use in practice, the one in this problem, the one from Problem 299, or the one from Problem 310?

313. The worst-case analysis of quicksort is often presented in class, but if not, then it makes a good exercise.

Chapter 7

Divide-and-Conquer

Divide-and-conquer is perhaps the most commonly used algorithm design technique in computer science. Faced with a big problem P, divide it into smaller problems, solve these subproblems, and combine their solutions into a solution for P. But how do you solve the smaller problems? Simply divide each of the small problems into smaller problems, and keep doing this until the problems become so small that it is trivial to solve them. Sound like recursion? Not surprisingly, a recursive procedure is usually the easiest way of implementing divide-and-conquer.

7.1 MAXIMUM AND MINIMUM

The following is a divide-and-conquer algorithm for finding the maximum value in an array $S[1..n]$. The main body of the algorithm consists of a call to maximum$(1, n)$.

```
        function maximum(x, y)
          comment return maximum in S[x..y]
  1.      if y − x ≤ 1 then return(max(S[x], S[y]))
  2.      else
  3.        max1:=maximum(x, ⌊(x + y)/2⌋)
  4.        max2:=maximum(⌊(x + y)/2⌋ + 1, y)
  5.        return(max(max1,max2))
```

314. ☞ ✍ Prove that the algorithm is correct. You may assume that n is a power of 2.

315. ☞ ✍ Write down a recurrence relation for the worst-case number of comparisons used by maximum$(1, n)$. Solve this recurrence relation. You may assume that n is a power of 2.

316. ☞ ✍ What is the running time of maximum$(1, n)$? Explain your answer.

Most textbooks introduce divide-and-conquer using the MAXMIN problem, the problem of finding the largest and smallest values in an array of n values. It is usually described for n a power of 2. The following problems ask you to extend this to arbitrary n.

317. 🎓🎓 💡 Design and analyze a divide-and-conquer MAXMIN algorithm that uses $\lceil 3n/2 \rceil - 2$ comparisons for any $n \in \mathbb{N}$.

318. 🎓 Consider the following MAXMIN algorithm. How many comparisons does it use? Is it likely to be faster or slower than the divide-and-conquer algorithm in practice?

> **procedure** maxmin2(S)
>   **comment** computes maximum and minimum of $S[1..n]$
>   in max and min resp.
> 1.   **if** n is odd **then** max:=$S[n]$; min:=$S[n]$
> 2.   **else** max:=$-\infty$; min:=∞
> 3.   **for** $i := 1$ to $\lfloor n/2 \rfloor$ **do**
> 4.   **if** $S[2i-1] \le S[2i]$
> 5.   **then** small:=$S[2i-1]$; large:=$S[2i]$
> 6.   **else** small:=$S[2i]$; large:=$S[2i-1]$
> 7.   **if** small < min **then** min:=small
> 8.   **if** large > max **then** min:=small

319. 🎓🎓 Show that any comparison-based MAXMIN algorithm must use at least $\lceil 3n/2 \rceil - 2$ comparisons in the worst case, for all $n \in \mathbb{N}$.

7.2 INTEGER MULTIPLICATION

Another popular example of divide-and-conquer is the $O(n^{1.59})$ time integer multiplication algorithm. The following questions will test your understanding of this algorithm and its analysis.

320. 🎓 What is the depth of recursion of the divide-and-conquer integer multiplication algorithm? At what depth does it start to repeat the same subproblems?

321. 🎓🎓 Suppose you are to write an algorithm for multiplying two n-bit integers, and you are told that you have a computer with word size $\sqrt{n}$, and hence that you can multiply two $\sqrt{n}$-bit integers in $O(1)$ time. Show that, by using the divide-and-conquer multiplication and stopping the recursion early, you can multiply two n-bit integers in time $O(n^{1.2925})$.

322. 🎓 Devise an algorithm to multiply an n-bit integer by an m-bit integer, where $n \ge m$, in time $O(nm^{\log 3 - 1})$.

Complete the design of the following algorithm for performing integer multiplication in time $O(n^{1.63})$. (This is slower than the standard algorithm, but its verification and analysis will test your abilities.) We use a technique similar to the standard divide-and-conquer algorithm. Instead of dividing the inputs y and z into two parts, we divide them into three parts. Suppose y and z have n bits, where n is a power of 3. Break y into three parts, a, b, c, each with $n/3$ bits. Break z into three parts, d, e, f, each with $n/3$ bits. Then,

$$yz = ad2^{4n/3} + (ae + bd)2^n + (af + cd + be)2^{2n/3} + (bf + ce)2^{n/3} + cf.$$

This can be computed as follows:

$$
\begin{aligned}
r_1 &:= ad \\
r_2 &:= (a+b)(d+e) \\
r_3 &:= be \\
r_4 &:= (a+c)(d+f) \\
r_5 &:= cf \\
r_6 &:= (b+c)(e+f) \\
x &:= r_1 2^{4n/3} + (r_2 - r_1 - r_3)2^n + (r_3 + r_4 - r_1 - r_5)2^{2n/3} \\
&\quad + (r_6 - r_3 - r_5)2^{n/3} + r_5.
\end{aligned}
$$

323. ☞ Show that $x = yz$.

324. ☞ ☀ Show that this algorithm runs in $O(n^{1.63})$ bit-operations, as claimed.

Joe D. Student is confused. He was told to implement the divide-and-conquer algorithm for integer multiplication, and find the value of n for which the divide-and-conquer algorithm is faster than the naive algorithm (see Problem 252) on n-bit integers. It must be faster for large enough n since, as he saw in class, the naive algorithm takes time $O(n^2)$ and the divide-and-conquer algorithm takes time $O(n^{1.585})$. Here is the Pascal data structure that he used:

```
const Precision=5000;
type Bit=0..1;
     longinteger=packed array[1..Precision] of Bit;
```

He started by writing procedures to do addition, left-shifting, and so on. For example, here is his addition procedure:

```
procedure LongAdd(var result,summand:longinteger);
  {result:=result+summand}
  var index,digitsum:integer;
```

```
      carry:Bit;
begin{LongAdd}
  carry:=0;
  for index:=1 to Precision do
    begin{for}
      digitsum:=result[index]+summand[index]+carry;
      carry:=digitsum div 2;
      result[index]:=digitsum mod 2;
    end;{for}
  if carry>0 then LongError(LongOverflow)
end;{LongAdd}
```

Joe carefully implemented the naive multiplication algorithm from Problem 252 as procedure LongMultiply, and the divide-and-conquer multiplication algorithm as procedure FastLongMultiply. Both of these procedures worked perfectly. However, he found that LongMultiply was faster than FastLongMultiply, even when he tried multiplying $2^n - 1$ by itself (which is guaranteed to make LongMultiply slow). Joe's data show that as n increases, FastLongMultiply becomes slower than LongMultiply by more than a constant factor. Figure 7.1 shows his running times, and Figure 7.2 their ratio.

325. ☞ Show that the worst case for the naive integer multiplication algorithm is, as claimed above, multiplying $2^n - 1$ by itself.

326. ☞ ☀ What did Joe do wrong?

327. ☞ What can Joe do to fix his program so that FastLongMultiply is faster than LongMultiply for large enough n?

Complete the design of the following algorithm for performing integer multiplication using $O(n^{1.585}/(\log n)^{0.585})$ bit-operations. First, construct a table of all k-bit products. To multiply two n-bit numbers, do the following. Perform the divide-and-conquer algorithm with the base of recursion $n \leq k$. That is, if $n \leq k$, then simply look up the result in the table. Otherwise, cut the numbers in half and perform the recursion as normal.

328. ☞ Show that a table of all k-bit products can be constructed using $O(k4^k)$ bit-operations.

329. ☞ ☺☞ Devise and solve a recurrence relation for the divide-and-conquer multiplication algorithm when the base of recursion is $T(n) = O(1)$ for all $n \leq k$. Your solution must be a function of both n and k.

330. ☞ ☞ ☺☞ Show that the best value of k is $\Theta(\log n)$, and that this gives an algorithm that uses $O(n^{1.585}/(\log n)^{0.585})$ bit-operations, as claimed.

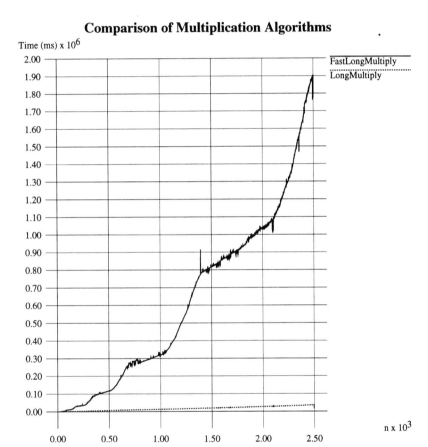

Figure 7.1. Running times for procedures LongMultiply and FastLongMultiply observed by Joe D. Student.

Ratio of Running Times

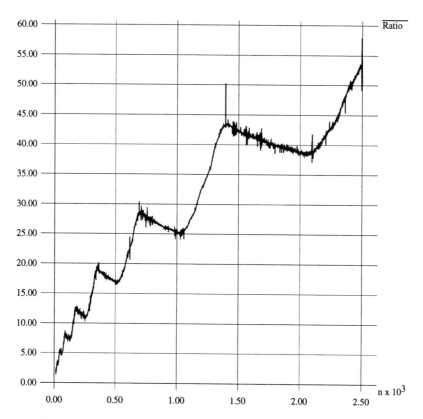

Figure 7.2. The ratio of the running times for procedures LongMultiply and FastLongMultiply observed by Joe D. Student.

7.3 STRASSEN'S ALGORITHM

Strassen's algorithm is a divide-and-conquer algorithm for multiplying $n \times n$ matrices in time $O(n^{2.81})$. The key ideas behind the algorithm are that 2×2 matrices can be multiplied using only seven multiplications instead of the usual eight (see Problems 263 and 297), and that this can be used as the base of recursion in a divide-and-conquer algorithm.

331. ☞ The standard description of Strassen's algorithm assumes that n is a power of 2. Devise an algorithm that runs in time $O(n^{2.81})$ when n is not necessarily a power of 2.

332. ☞ Suppose we were to come up with a variant of Strassen's algorithm based on the fact that 3×3 matrices can be multiplied in only m multiplications instead of the normal 27. How small would m have to be for this algorithm to be faster than Strassen's algorithm for large enough n?

333. ☞ The current record for matrix multiplication is $O(n^{2.376})$, due to Coppersmith and Winograd [18]. How small would m need to be in Problem 332 in order to improve on this bound?

Another version of Strassen's algorithm uses the following identities. To compute

$$\begin{bmatrix} A & B \\ C & D \end{bmatrix} = \begin{bmatrix} E & F \\ G & H \end{bmatrix} \cdot \begin{bmatrix} I & J \\ K & L \end{bmatrix},$$

first compute the following values:

$$
\begin{array}{lll}
s_1 = G + H & m_1 = s_2 s_6 & t_1 = m_1 + m_2 \\
s_2 = s_1 - E & m_2 = EI & t_2 = t_1 + m_4 \\
s_3 = E - G & m_3 = FK & \\
s_4 = F - s_2 & m_4 = s_3 s_7 & \\
s_5 = J - I & m_5 = s_1 s_5 & \\
s_6 = L - s_5 & m_6 = s_4 L & \\
s_7 = L - J & m_7 = H s_8 & \\
s_8 = s_6 - K. & &
\end{array}
$$

Then,

$$
\begin{array}{rcl}
A & = & m_2 + m_3 \\
B & = & t_1 + m_5 + m_6 \\
C & = & t_2 - m_7 \\
D & = & t_2 + m_5.
\end{array}
$$

334. ☞ Prove that this algorithm is correct.

335. ☜ Analyze its running time. Is it likely to be faster or slower than the standard version of Strassen's algorithm in practice?

7.4   BINARY SEARCH

Binary search is a classic divide-and-conquer algorithm that is usually covered in more elementary courses, but deserves to be dusted off again for a brief inspection during the algorithms course. I usually teach it for n a power of 2, and leave the extension to general n as an exercise (Problem 336).

336. ☜ ☜ ☺☞ Show that the number of comparisons used by the binary search algorithm when n is not necessarily a power of 2 is at most $\lceil \log n \rceil$.

337. ☜ What is wrong with the following binary search algorithm?

> **function** search(A, x, ℓ, r)
> **comment** find x in $A[\ell..r]$
> **if** $\ell = r$ **then return**(ℓ)
>   **else**
> $m := \lfloor (\ell + r)/2 \rfloor$
>   **if** $x \le A[m]$
>   **then return**$(\text{search}(A, x, \ell, m))$
>   **else return**$(\text{search}(A, x, m, r))$

338. ☜ Is the following algorithm for binary search correct? If so, prove it. If not, give an example on which it fails.

> **function** search(A, x, ℓ, r)
> **comment** find x in $A[\ell..r]$
> **if** $\ell = r$ **then return**(ℓ)
>   **else**
> $m := \lfloor \ell + (r - \ell + 1)/2 \rfloor$
>   **if** $x \le A[m]$
>   **then return**$(\text{search}(A, x, \ell, m))$
>   **else return**$(\text{search}(A, x, m + 1, r))$

339. ☜ ☜ Do an exact analysis for the average number of comparisons used by binary search for successful searches, assuming that all elements in the sequence are accessed with equal probability.

340. ☜ ☜ Use the binary search technique to devise an algorithm for the problem of finding square-roots of natural numbers: Given an n-bit natural number N, compute $\lceil \sqrt{n} \rceil$ using only $O(n)$ additions and shifts.

The following problems ask you to modify binary search in some way. For each of them, write pseudocode for the algorithm, devise and solve a recurrence relation for the number of comparisons used, and analyze the running time of your algorithm.

341. ☞ Modify the binary search algorithm so that it splits the input not into two sets of almost-equal sizes, but into two sets of sizes approximately one-third and two-thirds.

342. ☞ Modify the binary search algorithm to give a ternary search algorithm that splits the input not into two sets of almost-equal sizes, but into three sets of sizes approximately one-third.

343. ☞ Let $T[1..n]$ be a sorted array of distinct integers. Give a divide-and-conquer algorithm that finds an index i such that $T[i] = i$ (if one exists) and runs in time $O(\log n)$.

7.5   QUICKSORT

The following is a high-level version of Hoare's quicksort algorithm. Suppose S is a set of numbers.

```
        function quicksort(S)
 1.        if |S| ≤ 1
 2.        then return(S)
 3.        else
 4.           Choose an element a from S
 5.           Let S₁, S₂, S₃ be the elements of S that are respectively <, =, > a
 6.           return(quicksort(S₁),S₂,quicksort(S₃))
```

The operation described in line 5 is known as *pivoting* on a.

344. ☞ The *median* of a set of n values is the $\lceil n/2 \rceil$th smallest value. Suppose quicksort were to always pivot on the median value. How many comparisons would be made then in the worst case?

345. ☞ Suppose quicksort were to always pivot on the $\lceil n/3 \rceil$th smallest value. How many comparisons would be made then in the worst case?

An α-*pseudomedian* of a list of n distinct values (where $0 < \alpha < 1$) is a value that has at least n^α list elements larger than it, and at least n^α list elements smaller than it. The following is a divide-and-conquer algorithm for computing a pseudomedian (that is, an α-pseudomedian for some value of α to be determined later). Assume

n is a power of 3. If $n = 3$, then simply sort the 3 values and return the median. Otherwise, divide the n items into $n/3$ groups of 3 values. Sort each group of 3, and pick out the $n/3$ medians. Now recursively apply the procedure to find a pseudomedian of these values.

346. ☞ Let $T(n)$ be the number of comparisons used by the preceding algorithm for computing a pseudomedian. Write a recurrence relation for $T(n)$, and solve it exactly. Hence, show that the algorithm runs in time $O(n)$.

347. ☞☞ Let $E(n)$ be the number of values that are smaller than the value found by the preceding algorithm. Write a recurrence relation for $E(n)$, and hence prove that the algorithm does return a pseudomedian. What is the value of α?

348. ☞☞ Any odd number can be used instead of 3. Is there any odd number less than 13 which is better? You may use the following table, which gives the minimum number of comparisons $S(n)$ needed to sort $n \leq 11$ numbers.

n	1	2	3	4	5	6	7	8	9	10	11
$S(n)$	0	1	3	5	7	10	13	16	19	22	26

349. ☞☞ ☺☞ Suppose the pseudomedian algorithm is used to find the pivot value in quicksort. Does it improve the worst-case number of comparisons made?

The following is an implementation of Quicksort on an array $S[1..n]$ due to Dijkstra [21]. You were asked to prove it correct in Problem 279 and analyze it in Problem 313.

```
1.    procedure quicksort(ℓ, r)
2.       comment sort S[ℓ..r]
3.       i := ℓ; j := r;
4.       a := some element from S[ℓ..r];
5.       repeat
6.          while S[i] < a do i := i + 1;
7.          while S[j] > a do j := j − 1;
8.          if i ≤ j then
9.             swap S[i] and S[j];
10.            i := i + 1; j := j − 1;
11.      until i > j;
12.      if ℓ < j then quicksort(ℓ, j);
13.      if i < r then quicksort(i, r);
```

350. ☞ How many comparisons does it use to sort n values in the worst case?

351. ☞☞ How many comparisons does it use to sort n values on average ?

352. ☞☞ Suppose the preceding algorithm pivots on the middle value, that is, line 4 is replaced by $a := S[\lfloor (\ell + r)/2 \rfloor]$. Give an input of 8 values for which quicksort exhibits its worst-case behavior.

353. ☞☞☞ Suppose the above algorithm pivots on the middle value, that is, line 4 is replaced by $a := S[\lfloor (\ell + r)/2 \rfloor]$. Give an input of n values for which quicksort exhibits its worst-case behavior.

7.6 TOWERS OF HANOI

The Towers of Hanoi problem is often used as an example of recursion in introductory programming courses. This problem can be resurrected later in an algorithms course, usually to good effect. You are given n disks of differing diameter, arranged in increasing order of diameter from top to bottom on the leftmost of three pegs. You are allowed to move a single disk at a time from one peg to another, but you must not place a larger disk on top of a smaller one. Your task is to move all disks to the rightmost peg via a sequence of these moves. The earliest reference to this problem known to the author is Édouard Lucas [55] in Graham, Knuth, and Patashnik [30].

354. ☞ 🗒 ☺ How many moves does the divide-and-conquer algorithm use?

355. ☞☞ 👤 🗒 Show that the following algorithm solves the Towers of Hanoi problem. Think of the pegs as being arranged in a circle, with clockwise moves being from peg 1 to peg 2 to peg 3 to peg 1. If n is odd, then start by moving the smallest disk one jump in the counterclockwise direction. Alternate between moving the smallest disk in this manner and the only other legal move available. If n is even, then start by moving the smallest disk one jump in the clockwise direction. Alternate between moving the smallest disk in this manner and the only other legal move available.

356. ☞ Prove that any algorithm that solves the Towers of Hanoi problem must make at least $2^n - 1$ moves.

Each of the following problems asks you to devise a divide-and-conquer algorithm for a variant of the Towers of Hanoi problem. Write pseudocode for each algorithm, prove that it is correct, and analyze the number of moves made.

357. ☞☞ 👤 Devise a divide-and-conquer algorithm for the Towers of Hanoi problem when moves between peg 1 and peg 3 are not allowed (that is, all moves must be either to or from peg 2).

358. ☞ Devise an efficient divide-and-conquer algorithm for the Towers of Hanoi problem when there are $2n$ disks of n different sizes, two of each size, and you are not allowed to put a larger disk on top of a smaller one (but you can put a disk on top of a same-size one).

359. ☞☞ ▯ Devise an efficient divide-and-conquer algorithm for the Towers of Hanoi problem when all moves must be in a clockwise direction (that is, from peg 1 to peg 2, from peg 2 to peg 3, or from peg 3 to peg 1.)

360. ☞☞ ☺⌐ Devise an efficient divide-and-conquer algorithm for the Towers of Hanoi problem that works when the disks are started in any legal position (and still moves all disks to peg 3). How many moves does your algorithm make?

361. ☞☞ ▯ Devise a divide-and-conquer algorithm for the Towers of Hanoi problem when there are four pegs, using at most $O(n2^{\sqrt{2n}})$ moves.

362. ☞☞ ▯ Devise a divide-and-conquer algorithm for the Towers of Hanoi problem when there are $k \geq 4$ pegs, using at most $O(\sqrt[w]{n^2} \cdot 2^{w \sqrt[w]{n}/\sqrt{2}})$ moves, where $w = k - 2$ is the number of work-pegs.

363. ☞☞ ▯ Devise an efficient divide-and-conquer algorithm for the Towers of Hanoi problem when the disks are colored alternately red and blue, and we add the extra rule that no disk may be placed on any other disk of the same color.

7.7 DEPTH-FIRST SEARCH

Depth-first search is a search technique for directed graphs. Among its many applications, finding connected components of a directed graph and biconnected components of an undirected graph are the ones most commonly covered in algorithms courses. Depth-first search is performed on a directed graph $G = (V, E)$ by executing the following procedure on some $v \in V$:

$$
\begin{aligned}
&\textbf{procedure } \mathrm{dfs}(v) \\
1. \quad &\quad \text{mark } v \text{ used} \\
2. \quad &\quad \textbf{for } \text{each } w \in V \text{ such that } (v, w) \in E \textbf{ do} \\
3. \quad &\quad\quad \textbf{if } w \text{ is unused } \textbf{then} \\
4. \quad &\quad\quad\quad \text{mark } (v, w) \text{ used} \\
5. \quad &\quad\quad\quad \mathrm{dfs}(w)
\end{aligned}
$$

The set of marked edges form a *depth-first spanning tree* of a connected component of G.

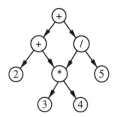

Figure 7.3. A DAG representing the arithmetic expression
$2 + 3 * 4 + 5/(3 * 4)$.

364. ☞ Suppose an arithmetic expression is given as a DAG (directed acyclic graph) with common subexpressions removed. For example, the expression $2 + 3 * 4 + 5/(3 * 4)$ would be given as the DAG shown in Figure 7.3. Devise an algorithm for evaluating such a DAG with out-degree 2 (that is, all vertices have at most 2 outgoing edges) in time $O(n)$.

365. ☞☞ ☀ An undirected graph $G = (V, E)$ is said to be *k-colorable* if all the vertices of G can be colored using k different colors such that no two adjacent vertices have the same color. Design an algorithm that runs in time $O(n + e)$ to color a graph with two colors or determine that the graph is not 2-colorable.

366. ☞☞ A *triangle* in an undirected graph $G = (V, E)$ is a set of three pairwise distinct vertices $u, v, w \in V$ such that $(u, v) \in E$, $(v, w) \in E$, and $(u, w) \in E$. Design an algorithm to test whether an undirected graph has a triangle. If G has n vertices and e edges, then your algorithm should run in time $O(n + e)$.

367. ☞☞ Design an algorithm that, given a directed graph $G = (V, E)$ and a distinguished vertex $s \in V$, determines for each $v \in V$ the shortest path from s to v. If G has n vertices and e edges, then your algorithm must run in time $O(n + e)$.

368. ☞☞ ☀ A *forest* is a graph composed of zero or more disconnected trees. Design an algorithm that, given a graph G with n nodes, determines whether G is a forest in time $O(n)$.

7.8 APPLICATIONS

The following problems ask you to solve new problems using divide-and-conquer. For each of your algorithms, describe it in prose or pseudocode, prove it correct, and analyze its running time.

369. ⚐⚐⚐ 💡 🖙 ☺⌐ Devise a divide-and-conquer algorithm for constructing a closed knight's tour on an $n \times n$ chessboard for all even $n \geq 6$ (see
Problem 48 for definitions). Your algorithm must run in time $O(n^2)$.

370. ⚐ ☺⌐ The *longest ascending subsequence problem* is defined as follows.
Given an array $A[1..n]$ of natural numbers, find the length of the longest
ascending subsequence of A. (A *subsequence* is a list $A[i_1], A[i_2], \ldots, A[i_m]$
for some $1 \leq i_1 < i_2 < \cdots < i_m \leq n$. The value m is called the *length* of
the subsequence. Such a subsequence is called *ascending* if $A[i_1] \leq A[i_2] \leq
\cdots \leq A[i_m]$.) Devise a divide-and-conquer algorithm for solving the longest
ascending subsequence problem in time $O(n^2)$.

371. ⚐⚐ ☺⌐ The *maximum subsequence sum* problem is defined as follows.
Given an array $A[1..n]$ of natural numbers, find values of i and j with $1 \leq i \leq
j \leq n$ such that

$$\sum_{k=i}^{j} A[k]$$

is maximized. Devise a divide-and-conquer algorithm for solving the maximum subsequence sum problem in time $O(n \log n)$.

372. ⚐ Devise a divide-and-conquer algorithm for multiplying n complex numbers using only $3(n-1)$ real multiplications.

373. ⚐⚐⚐ Suppose we are given a set of n numbers $k_1, \ldots, k_n$, where each
k_i has an associated weight $w_i \geq 0$ such that $\sum_{i=1}^{n} w_i = 1$. The weighted
median of the set $\{(k_i, w_i) \mid 1 \leq i \leq n\}$ is the number k_m such that

$$\sum_{k_l < k_m} w_l < \frac{1}{2}, \sum_{k_l \leq k_m} w_l \geq \frac{1}{2}.$$

For example, given

$$k_1 = 4.13, k_2 = 2.76, k_3 = 9.00, k_4 = 3.09, k_5 = 7.65,$$

$$w_1 = 0.30, w_2 = 0.15, w_3 = 0.25, w_4 = 0.10, w_5 = 0.20$$

the weighted median is $k_1 = 4.13$ because

$$\sum_{k_l < 4.13} w_l = w_2 + w_4 = 0.15 + 0.10 = 0.25,$$

$$\sum_{k_l \leq 4.13} w_l = w_2 + w_4 + w_1 = 0.15 + 0.10 + 0.30 = 0.55.$$

Design an efficient (that is, linear time) algorithm to find the weighted median. (Note that the k_is need not be given in sorted order.) Prove that your
algorithm performs as claimed.

374. ☞☞ 🎓 An *induced subgraph* of a graph $G = (V, E)$ is a graph $H = (U, F)$ such that $U \subseteq V$, and $F = E \cap (U \times U)$. Given an undirected graph $G = (V, E)$ and an integer k, find the maximum induced subgraph H of G such that each vertex in H has degree at least k, or determine that it does not exist. The algorithm should run in time $O(n + e)$.

375. ☞☞ 🎓 Find an algorithm that, given a connected graph in which all vertices have even degree, constructs an Eulerian cycle in time $O(n + e)$. (See also Problem 69.)

376. ☞☞ Let $G = (V, E)$ be a directed graph (not necessarily acyclic). Design an efficient algorithm to label the vertices of the graph with distinct labels from 1 to $|V|$ such that the label of each vertex v is greater than the label of at least one of v's predecessors (if v has any), or to determine that no such labeling is possible (w is a *predecessor* of v iff $(w, v) \in E$). Your algorithm should run in time $O(n + e)$.

377. ☞☞ Given two sorted sequences with m, n elements, respectively, design and analyze an efficient divide-and-conquer algorithm to find the kth element in the merge of the two sequences. The best algorithm runs in time $O(\log(\max(m, n)))$.

7.9   HINTS

317. Separate the n numbers into disjoint subsets (finding the right decomposition is crucial) and first run the known recursive algorithm on the subsets.

324. Observe that x is computed using only six multiplications of $n/3$-bit integers, plus some additions and shifts. Solve the resulting recurrence relation.

326. Start by deriving and solving a recurrence relation for the number of times that Joe's procedure LongAdd is called by procedures LongMultiply and Fast-LongMultiply.

355. Show that this algorithm makes exactly the same moves as the standard divide-and-conquer algorithm.

357. No, it is not enough to use the standard algorithm and replace every move from peg 1 to peg 3 (for example) with two moves to and from peg 2. That may require you to place a large disk on top of a small one.

359. No, it is not enough to use the standard algorithm and replace every counter-clockwise move with two clockwise moves. That may require you to place a large disk on top of a small one. It is possible to devise a divide-and-conquer

algorithm for moving all of the disks one peg clockwise using $(4^n-1)/3$ moves. This can be used to solve the Towers of Hanoi problem (which is to move all of the disks one peg counterclockwise) in $2(4^n-1)/3$ moves. The best algorithm known to the author uses less than $(1+\sqrt{3})^n - 1 = O(2.73^n)$ moves.

361. An analysis of a k-peg algorithm by Lu [54] can be found in in Veerasamy and Page [81]. We are interested in the case $k = 4$, which slightly simplifies the analysis. In addition, the analysis is much simpler if you prove it by induction. If you try to pass off their analysis as your own, it is long enough and idiosyncratic enough that your instructor will be sure to recognize it.

362. An algorithm by Lu [54] was shown to use at most $n2^{\sqrt[w]{w!\cdot n}}$ moves by Veerasamy and Page [81]. (If you read their paper, note that their k is the number of work pegs, which is w in our notation.) The algorithm that I have in mind has recurrence $T(k,n) = T(k/2+1, \sqrt{n})^2$.

363. Surprisingly, the standard algorithm solves this problem. You can prove it by induction on n, but be careful about the bottom disk on each peg. The induction hypothesis will have to be stronger than just the statement of the required result. To get the idea, play with some examples.

365. Take note of which section this problem is in.

368. It's easy to do this in time $O(n+e)$, but that is not what is asked for. A problem from Chapter 2 is relevant.

369. In order to construct closed knight's tours on square chessboards, you will need a method for constructing tours on rectangular boards. If you are smart enough, you will only need $n \times (n+2)$ tours. You will also need some extra structure in your tours to enable them to be joined at the corners (see Problem 48). You will have to devise an exhaustive search algorithm for finding small tours for the base of your divide-and-conquer (see Problem 513), or you can make use of the tours shown in Figure 7.4.

374. Use the adjacency list representation. Store for each $v \in V$ an additional field called its *degree*. Start by giving an algorithm that sets this field to the correct value. Then write a divide-and-conquer algorithm that, given a vertex v of degree less than k, deletes that vertex from the graph, and all vertices of degree less than k that are adjacent to it. Apply this algorithm to solve the required problem.

375. See Problem 69.

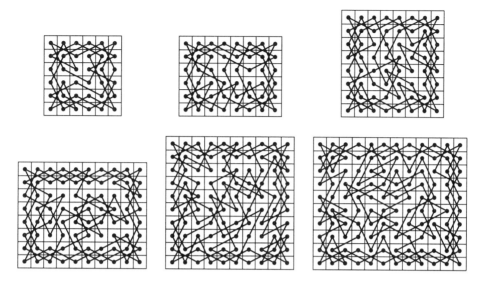

Figure 7.4. Knight's tours for (in row-major order) 6×6,
6×8, 8×8, 8×10, 10×10, and 10×12 boards.

7.10   SOLUTIONS

314. Here is a full solution when n is not necessarily a power of 2. The size of
the problem is the number of entries in the array, $y - x + 1$. We will prove
by induction on $n = y - x + 1$ that maximum(x, y) will return the maximum
value in $S[x..y]$. The algorithm is clearly correct when $n \leq 2$. Now suppose
$n > 2$, and that maximum(x, y) will return the maximum value in $S[x..y]$
whenever $y - x + 1 < n$. In order to apply the induction hypothesis to the
first recursive call, we must prove that $\lfloor (x + y)/2 \rfloor - x + 1 < n$. There are
two cases to consider. If $y - x + 1$ is even, then $y - x$ is odd, and hence $y + x$
is odd. Therefore,

$$\left\lfloor \frac{x + y}{2} \right\rfloor - x + 1 = \frac{x + y - 1}{2} - x + 1 = \frac{y - x + 1}{2} = \frac{n}{2} < n.$$

(The last inequality holds since $n > 2$.) If $y - x + 1$ is odd, then $y - x$ is even,
and hence $y + x$ is even. Therefore,

$$\left\lfloor \frac{x + y}{2} \right\rfloor - x + 1 = \frac{x + y}{2} - x + 1 = \frac{y - x + 2}{2} = \frac{n + 1}{2} < n.$$

(The last inequality holds since $n > 1$.) In order to apply the induction
hypothesis to the second recursive call, we must prove that $y - (\lfloor (x+y)/2 \rfloor +$

1) $+1 < n$. There are two cases to consider. If $y - x + 1$ is even, then

$$y - \left(\left\lfloor \frac{x+y}{2} \right\rfloor + 1\right) + 1 = y - \frac{x+y-1}{2} = \frac{y-x+1}{2} = \frac{n}{2} < n.$$

If $y - x + 1$ is odd, then

$$y - \left(\left\lfloor \frac{x+y}{2} \right\rfloor + 1\right) + 1 = y - \frac{x+y}{2} = \frac{y-x+1}{2} - 1/2 = \frac{n}{2} - \frac{1}{2} < n.$$

Procedure maximum divides the array into two parts. By the induction hypothesis, the recursive calls correctly find the maxima in these parts. Therefore, since the procedure returns the maximum of the two maxima, it returns the correct values.

315. Let $T(n)$ be the number of comparisons used by maximum(x, y), where $n = y - x + 1$ is the size of the array chunk processed. Then if n is a power of 2, $T(1) = 0$, and for all $n > 1$ a power of 2, $T(n) = 2T(n/2) + 1$. Hence, using the techniques of Chapter 4, $T(n) = n - 1$.

316. The running time of procedure maximum is clearly a constant times the number of comparisons. Hence, by the preceding, it runs in time $O(n)$.

354. Let $T(n)$ be the number of moves it takes to move n disks from peg i to peg j. Clearly,

$$T(n) = \begin{cases} 1 & \text{if } n = 1 \\ 2T(n-1) + 1 & \text{otherwise.} \end{cases}$$

Hence, using the techniques of Chapter 4, $T(n) = 2^n - 1$.

355. Let D be a direction, either clockwise or counterclockwise. Let $\overline{D}$ be the opposite direction. To move n disks in direction D, we are told to alternate between the following two moves:

- If n is odd, move the smallest disk in direction D. If n is even, move the smallest disk in direction $\overline{D}$.
- Make the only other legal move.

We claim that when the recursive algorithm is used to move n disks in direction D, it alternates between the preceding two moves. This is enough to prove correctness of the new algorithm. The proof of the claim is by induction on n. The claim is obviously true when $n = 1$. Now suppose that the claim is true for n disks. Suppose we use the recursive algorithm to move $n + 1$ disks in direction D. It does the following:

- Move n disks in direction $\overline{D}$.
- Move one disk in direction D.
- Move n disks in direction $\overline{D}$.

Let

- "D" denote moving the smallest disk in direction D,
- "$\overline{D}$" denote moving the smallest disk in direction $\overline{D}$, and
- "O" denote making the only other legal move.

Case 1. $n + 1$ is odd. Then n is even, and so by the induction hypothesis, moving n disks in direction $\overline{D}$ uses moves:

$$DODO \cdots OD.$$

(Note that by Problem 354, the number of moves is odd, so the preceding sequence of moves ends with D, not O.) Hence, moving $n+1$ disks in direction D uses

$$\underbrace{DODO \cdots OD}_{n \text{ disks}} O \underbrace{DODO \cdots OD}_{n \text{ disks}},$$

as required.

Case 2. $n + 1$ is even. Then n is odd, and so by the induction hypothesis, moving n disks in direction $\overline{D}$ uses moves

$$\overline{D}O\overline{D}O \cdots O\overline{D}.$$

(Note that by Problem 354, the number of moves is odd, so the preceding sequence of moves ends with $\overline{D}$, not O.) Hence, moving $n+1$ disks in direction D uses moves:

$$\underbrace{\overline{D}O\overline{D}O \cdots O\overline{D}}_{n \text{ disks}} O \underbrace{\overline{D}O\overline{D}O \cdots O\overline{D}}_{n \text{ disks}},$$

as required. Hence, by induction, the claim holds for any number of disks.

369. A solution to this problem appears in Parberry [62].

7.11 COMMENTS

321. See also Problem 329.

329. See also Problem 321.

330. So where does this algorithm get its speed from? The secret is in Problem 320. Although it is faster than the standard divide-and-conquer, there is a faster algorithm than this one (see Schönhage and Strassen [70]).

336. Binary search is normally described and analyzed for n a power of 2. This problem asks you to extend this to any value of n.

349. I don't propose this as a viable alternative to quicksort. This is just an exercise in the design, correctness proof, and analysis of divide-and-conquer algorithms.

354. According to legend, there is a set of 64 gold disks on 3 diamond needles being solved by priests of Brahma. The Universe is supposed to end when the task is complete. If done correctly, it will take $T(64) = 2^{64} - 1 = 1.84 \times 10^{19}$ moves. At one move per second, that's 5.85×10^{11} years. More realistically, at 1 minute per move (since the largest disks must be very heavy) during working hours, it would take 1.54×10^{14} years. The current age of the Universe is estimated at $\approx 10^{10}$ years. Perhaps the legend is correct.

360. There is an algorithm that will do this using at most $2^n - 1$ moves. There is even one that is provably optimal.

369. Alternative algorithms for constructing closed knight's tours on rectangular chessboards appear in Cull and DeCurtins [20] and Schwenk [71].

370. There is a faster algorithm for this problem. See Problem 409.

371. There is an $O(n)$ time algorithm for this problem.

Chapter 8

Dynamic Programming

Dynamic programming is a fancy name for divide-and-conquer with a table. Instead of solving subproblems recursively, solve them sequentially and store their solutions in a table. The trick is to solve them in the right order so that whenever the solution to a subproblem is needed, it is already available in the table. Dynamic programming is particularly useful on problems for which divide-and-conquer appears to yield an exponential number of subproblems, but there are really only a small number of subproblems repeated exponentially often. In this case, it makes sense to compute each solution the first time and store it away in a table for later use, instead of recomputing it recursively every time it is needed.

In general, I don't approve of busy-work problems, but I have found that undergraduates don't really understand dynamic programming unless they fill in a few tables for themselves. Hence, the following problems include a few of this nature.

8.1 ITERATED MATRIX PRODUCT

The iterated matrix product problem is perhaps the most popular example of dynamic programming used in algorithms texts. Given n matrices, $M_1, M_2, \ldots, M_n$, where for $1 \leq i \leq n$, M_i is a $r_{i-1} \times r_i$ matrix, parenthesize the product $M_1 \cdot M_2 \cdots M_n$ so as to minimize the total cost, assuming that the cost of multiplying an $r_{i-1} \times r_i$ matrix by a $r_i \times r_{i+1}$ matrix using the naive algorithm is $r_{i-1} r_i r_{i+1}$. (See also Problems 91 and 263.) Here is the dynamic programming algorithm for the matrix product problem:

```
function matrix(n)
1.    for i := 1 to n do m[i, i] := 0
2.    for d := 1 to n − 1 do
3.        for i := 1 to n − d do
4.            j := i + d
5.            m[i, j] := min_{i≤k<j}(m[i, k] + m[k + 1, j] + r_{i-1}r_k r_j)
6.    return(m[1, n])
```

378. ☞ 🔦 Find three other orders in which the cost table m can be filled in (ignoring the diagonal).

379. ☞ Prove that there are $\Omega(2^n)$ different orders in which the cost table m can be filled in.

Fill in the cost table m in the dynamic programming algorithm for iterated matrix products on the following inputs:

380. ☞ ☺ $n = 4$; $r_0 = 2$, $r_1 = 5$, $r_2 = 4$, $r_3 = 1$, $r_4 = 10$.

381. ☞ $n = 4$; $r_0 = 3$, $r_1 = 7$, $r_2 = 2$, $r_3 = 5$, $r_4 = 10$.

382. ☞ $n = 5$; $r_0 = 12$, $r_1 = 2$, $r_2 = 15$, $r_3 = 16$, $r_4 = 8$, $r_5 = 3$.

383. ☞ ✍ $n = 5$; $r_0 = 8$, $r_1 = 3$, $r_2 = 2$, $r_3 = 19$, $r_4 = 18$, $r_5 = 7$.

Find counterexamples to the following algorithms for the iterated matrix products problem. That is, find n, $r_0, r_1, \ldots, r_n$ such that, when the product of the matrices with these dimensions is evaluated in the order given, the cost is higher than optimal.

384. ☞ ✍ Suppose $n > 2$, and that r_i is the smallest of $r_1, r_2, \ldots, r_{n-1}$. Break the product after M_i, and recursively apply this procedure to the products $M_1 \times M_2 \times \cdots \times M_i$ and $M_{i+1} \times M_2 \times \cdots \times M_n$.

385. ☞ Multiply left to right.

386. ☞ Multiply right to left.

387. ☞ Start by cutting the product in half, and then repeat the same thing recursively in each half.

388. ☞ Suppose r_i is the largest of $r_1, r_2, \ldots, r_{n-1}$. Start by multiplying M_i by M_{i+1}. Repeat this until the product has been evaluated.

389. ☞ Suppose r_i is the smallest of $r_1, r_2, \ldots, r_{n-1}$. Start by multiplying M_i by M_{i+1}. Repeat this until the product has been evaluated.

390. ☞ Suppose r_i is the largest of $r_1, r_2, \ldots, r_{n-1}$. Break the product after M_i, and recursively apply this procedure to the products $M_1 \times M_2 \times \cdots \times M_i$ and $M_{i+1} \times M_2 \times \cdots \times M_n$.

8.2 THE KNAPSACK PROBLEM

The *knapsack problem* (often called the *zero-one knapsack problem*) is as follows: given n rods of length $s_1, s_2, \ldots, s_n$, and a natural number S, find a subset of the rods that has total length exactly S. The standard dynamic programming algorithm for the knapsack problem is as follows. Let $t[i, j]$ be **true** if there is a subset of the first i items that has total length exactly j.

$$\textbf{function } \mathrm{knapsack}(s_1, s_2, \ldots, s_n, S)$$

1. $t[0, 0] :=$**true**
2.   **for** $j := 1$ **to** S **do** $t[0, j] :=$**false**
3.   **for** $i := 1$ **to** n **do**
4.   **for** $j := 0$ **to** S **do**
5. $t[i, j] := t[i - 1, j]$
6.   **if** $j - s_i \geq 0$ **then** $t[i, j] := t[i, j] \lor t[i - 1, j - s_i]$
7.   **return**$(t[n, S])$

391. ☞ Fill in the table t in the dynamic programming algorithm for the knapsack problem on a knapsack of size 19 with rods of the following lengths: $15, 5, 16, 7, 1, 15, 6, 3$.

Fill in the table t in the dynamic programming algorithm for the knapsack problem on a knapsack of size 10 with rods of the following lengths:

392. ☞ 1, 2, 3, 4.

393. ☞ 5, 4, 3, 6.

394. ☞ 2, 2, 3, 3.

Find counterexamples to the following algorithms for the knapsack problem. That is, find S, n, $s_1, \ldots, s_n$ such that when the rods are selected using the algorithm given, the knapsack is not completely full.

395. ☞ Put them in the knapsack in left to right order (the first-fit algorithm).

396. ☞ Put them in smallest first (the best-fit algorithm).

397. ☞ Put them in largest first (the worst-fit algorithm).

8.3 OPTIMAL BINARY SEARCH TREES

Binary search trees are useful for storing a set S of ordered elements, with operations:

$$\begin{aligned}
&\text{search}(x, S): &&\text{return } \textbf{true} \text{ iff } x \in S,\\
&\min(S): &&\text{return the smallest value in } S,\\
&\text{delete}(x, S): &&\text{delete } x \text{ from } S,\\
&\text{insert}(x, S): &&\text{insert } x \text{ into } S.
\end{aligned}$$

The *optimal binary search tree problem* is the following. Given the following three sets of data,

1. $S = \{x_1, \ldots x_n\}$, where $x_i < x_{i+1}$ for all $1 \le i < n$,
2. the probability p_i that we will be asked member(x_i, S), for $1 \le i \le n$,
3. the probability q_i that we will be asked member(x, S) for some $x_i < x < x_{i+1}$ (where $x_0 = -\infty$, $x_{n+1} = \infty$), for $0 \le i \le n$,

construct a binary search tree (see also Section 11.2) that has the minimum number of expected comparisons.

The standard dynamic programming algorithm for this problem is as follows. Let $T_{i,j}$ be the min-cost binary search tree for $x_{i+1}, \ldots, x_j$, and $c[i,j]$ be the expected number of comparisons for $T_{i,j}$.

$$\begin{aligned}
&\textbf{function } \text{bst}(p_1, p_2, \ldots, p_n, q_0, q_1, \ldots, q_n)\\
&1.\quad \textbf{for } i := 0 \textbf{ to } n \textbf{ do}\\
&2.\qquad w[i,i] := q_i; \; c[i,i] := 0\\
&3.\quad \textbf{for } \ell := 1 \textbf{ to } n \textbf{ do}\\
&4.\qquad \textbf{for } i := 0 \textbf{ to } n - \ell \textbf{ do}\\
&5.\qquad\quad j := i + \ell\\
&6.\qquad\quad w[i,j] := w[i,j-1] + p_j + q_j\\
&7.\qquad\quad c[i,j] := \min_{i<k\le j}(c[i,k-1] + c[k,j] + w[i,j])\\
&8.\quad \textbf{return}(c[0,n])
\end{aligned}$$

Fill in the cost table c in the dynamic programming algorithm for the optimal binary search tree problem on the following inputs.

398. ⚓ $n = 4$, $p_1 = 0.01$, $p_2 = 0.11$, $p_3 = 0.2$, $p_4 = 0.12$; $q_0 = 0.1$, $q_1 = 0.1$, $q_2 = 0.28$, $q_3 = 0.03$, $q_4 = 0.05$.

399. ⚓ $n = 4$, $p_1 = 0.15$, $p_2 = 0.32$, $p_3 = 0.02$, $p_4 = 0.07$; $q_0 = 0.01$, $q_1 = 0.16$, $q_2 = 0.21$, $q_3 = 0.02$, $q_4 = 0.04$.

400. ⚓ $n = 4$, $p_1 = 0.07$, $p_2 = 0.22$, $p_3 = 0.07$, $p_4 = 0.17$; $q_0 = 0.03$, $q_1 = 0.03$, $q_2 = 0.21$, $q_3 = 0.09$, $q_4 = 0.12$.

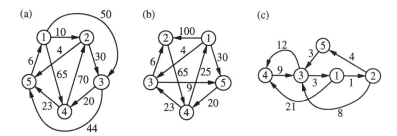

Figure 8.1. Some graphs.

8.4 FLOYD'S ALGORITHM

The *all-pairs shortest-paths* problem is as follows. Given a labeled directed graph
$G = (V, E)$, find for each pair of vertices $v, w \in V$ the cost of the shortest (that
is, the least-cost) path from v to w in G. The standard dynamic programming
algorithm for the all pairs shortest paths problem (Floyd's algorithm) is as follows.
Suppose $V = \{1, 2, \ldots, n\}$.

> **function** floyd(C, n)
> 1.   **for** $i := 1$ **to** n **do**
> 2.   **for** $j := 1$ **to** n **do**
> 3.   **if** $(i, j) \in E$
> 4.   **then** $A[i, j] :=$ cost of edge (i, j)
> 5.   **else** $A[i, j] := \infty$
> 6. $A[i, i] := 0$
> 7.   **for** $k := 1$ **to** n **do**
> 8.   **for** $i := 1$ **to** n **do**
> 9.   **for** $j := 1$ **to** n **do**
> 10.   **if** $A[i, k] + A[k, j] < A[i, j]$ **then** $A[i, j] := A[i, k] + A[k, j]$
> 11.   **return**(A)

401. 🎓 Fill in the cost table A in Floyd's algorithm on the graphs shown in
      Figure 8.1.

402. 🎓🎓 Show that Floyd's algorithm on an undirected graph chooses a mini-
      mum cost edge (v, w) for each vertex v. Can an all-pairs shortest-path algo-
      rithm be designed simply by choosing such a cheapest edge for each vertex?
      What if all edge costs are different?

Modify Floyd's algorithm to solve the following problems on directed graphs. Analyze your algorithms.

403. ☞☞ Determine the number of paths (possibly infinite) between each pair of vertices.

404. ☞☞ Determine the number of even-length paths and of odd-length paths between each pair of vertices.

405. ☞☞ Determine the number of shortest paths between each pair of vertices.

406. ☞☞ Given an n-vertex graph whose vertices are labeled with distinct integers from 1 to n, the label of each path is obtained by taking the labels of vertices on the path in order. Determine the label and length of the lexicographically first shortest path between each pair of vertices.

8.5 APPLICATIONS

The problems in this section ask you to apply dynamic programming in new situations. One way to proceed is to start by devising a divide-and-conquer algorithm, replace the recursion with table lookups, and devise a series of loops that fill in the table in the correct order.

407. ☞☞ A *context-free grammar* in Chomsky Normal Form consists of

   - A set of *nonterminal symbols* N.
   - A set of *terminal symbols* T.
   - A special nonterminal symbol called the *root*.
   - A set of *productions* of the form either $A \to BC$, or $A \to a$, where $A, B, C \in N$, $a \in T$.

If $A \in N$, define $\mathcal{L}(A)$ as follows:

$$\mathcal{L}(A) = \{bc \mid b \in \mathcal{L}(B), c \in \mathcal{L}(C), \text{ where } A \to BC\} \cup \{a \mid A \to a\}.$$

The *language* generated by a grammar with root R is defined to be $\mathcal{L}(R)$. The *CFL recognition problem* is the following: For a fixed context-free grammar in Chomsky Normal Form, on input a string of terminals x, determine whether x is in the language generated by the grammar. Devise an algorithm for the CFL recognition problem. Analyze your algorithm.

408. ☞ Fill in the tables in the dynamic programming algorithm for the CFL recognition problem (see Problem 407) on the following inputs. In each case, the root symbol is S.

   (a) ☞ Grammar: $S \to SS$, $S \to s$. String: *ssssss*.

   (b) ☞ Grammar: $S \to AR$, $S \to AB$, $A \to a$, $R \to SB$, $B \to b$. String: *aaabbb*.

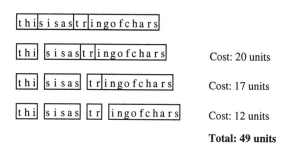

Figure 8.2. The cost of making the breaks in left-to-right order.

(c) ☞ Grammar: $S \rightarrow AX$, $X \rightarrow SA$, $A \rightarrow a$, $S \rightarrow BY$, $Y \rightarrow SB$, $B \rightarrow b$, $S \rightarrow CZ$, $Z \rightarrow SC$, $C \rightarrow c$. String: *abacbbcaba*.

409. ☞ ☞ ☼ Devise a dynamic programming algorithm that solves the longest ascending subsequence (see Problem 370) in time $O(n \log n)$.

410. ☞ ☞ A certain string-processing language allows the programmer to break a string into two pieces. Since this involves copying the old string, it costs n units of time to break a string of n characters into two pieces. Suppose a programmer wants to break a string into many pieces. The order in which the breaks are made can affect the total amount of time used. For example, suppose we wish to break a 20 character string after characters 3, 8, and 10 (numbering the characters in ascending order from the left-hand end, starting from 1). If the breaks are made in left-to-right order, then the first breaks costs 20 units of time, the second breaks costs 17 units of time, and the third breaks costs 12 units of time, a total of 49 units of time (see Figure 8.2). If the breaks are made in right-to-left order, then the first break costs 20 units of time, the second break costs 10 units of time, and the third break costs 8 units of time, a total of 38 units of time (see Figure 8.3). Devise a dynamic programming algorithm that, when given the numbers of the characters after which to break, determines the cheapest cost of those breaks in time $O(n^3)$.

411. Find counterexamples to the following algorithms for the string-cutting problem introduced in Problem 410. That is, find the length of the string, and several places to cut such that when cuts are made in the order given, the cost in higher than optimal.

(a) ☞ Start by cutting the string as close to the middle as possible, and then repeat the same thing recursively in each half.

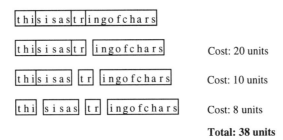

Figure 8.3. The cost of making the breaks in right-to-left order.

(b) ☞ Start by making (at most) two cuts to separate the smallest substring. Repeat this until finished. Start by making (at most) two cuts to separate the largest substring. Repeat this until finished.

412. ☞☞ There are two warehouses V and W from which widgets are to be shipped to destinations D_i, $1 \leq i \leq n$. Let d_i be the demand at D_i, for $1 \leq i \leq n$, and r_V, r_W be the number of widgets available at V and W, respectively. Assume that there are enough widgets available to fill the demand, that is, that

$$r_V + r_W = \sum_{i=1}^{n} d_i. \tag{8.1}$$

Let v_i be the cost of shipping a widget from warehouse V to destination D_i, and w_i be the cost of shipping a widget from warehouse W to destination D_i, for $1 \leq i \leq n$. The *warehouse problem* is the problem of finding $x_i, y_i \in \mathbb{N}$ for $1 \leq i \leq n$ such that when x_i widgets are sent from V to D_i and y_i widgets are sent from W to D_i:

- the demand at D_i is filled, that is, $x_i + y_i = d_i$,
- the inventory at V is sufficient, that is, $\sum_{i=1}^{n} x_i = r_V$,
- the inventory at W is sufficient, that is, $\sum_{i=1}^{n} y_i = r_W$,

and the total cost of shipping the widgets,

$$\sum_{i=1}^{n} (v_i x_i + w_i y_i)$$

is minimized.

(a) Let $g_j(x)$ be the cost incurred when V has an inventory of x widgets, and supplies are sent to destinations D_i for all $1 \leq i \leq j$ in the optimal

Advance	Move cursor one character to the right
Delete	Delete the character under the cursor, and move the cursor to the next character.
Replace	Replace the character under the cursor with another. The cursor remains stationary.
Insert	Insert a new character before the one under the cursor. The cursor remains stationary.
Kill	Delete all characters from (and including) the one under the cursor to the end of the line. This can only be the last operation.

Table 8.1. Operations allowed on a smart terminal.

manner (note that W is not mentioned because knowledge of the inventory for V implies knowledge of the inventory for W, by (8.1).) Write a recurrence relation for $g_j(x)$ in terms of g_{j-1}.

(b) Use this recurrence to devise a dynamic programming algorithm that finds the cost of the cheapest solution to the warehouse problem. Analyze your algorithm.

413. ☞ ☞ ☼ Consider the problem of neatly printing a paragraph of text on a printer with fixed-width fonts. The input text is a sequence of n words containing $\ell_1, \ell_2, \ldots, \ell_n$, characters, respectively. Each line on the printer can hold up to M characters. If a printed line contains words i through j, then the number of blanks left at the end of the line (given that there is one blank between each pair of words) is

$$M - j + i - \sum_{k=i}^{j} \ell_k.$$

We wish to minimize the sum, over all lines except the last, of the cubes of the number of blanks at the end of each line (for example, if there are k lines with $b_1, b_2, \ldots, b_k$ blanks at the ends, respectively, then we wish to minimize $b_1^3 + b_2^3 + \cdots + b_{k-1}^3$). Give a dynamic programming algorithm to compute this value. Analyze your algorithm.

414. ☞ ☞ A "smart" terminal changes one string displayed on the screen into another by a series of simple operations. The cursor is initially on the first character of the string. The operations are shown in Table 8.1. For example, one way to transform the string `algorithm` to the string `altruistic` is shown in Figure 8.4.

Operation	String
	Algorithm
advance	aLgorithm
advance	alGorithm
replace with t	alTorithm
advance	altOrithm
delete	altRithm
advance	altrIthm
insert u	altruIthm
advance	altruiThm
insert s	altruisThm
advance	altruistHm
insert i	altruistiHm
insert c	altruisticHm
kill	altruistic

Figure 8.4. Transforming algorithm to altruistic using the operations shown in Table 8.1. The cursor position is indicated by a capital letter.

There are many sequences of operations that achieve the same result. Suppose that on a particular brand of terminal, the advance operation takes a milliseconds, the delete operation takes d milliseconds, the replace operation takes r milliseconds, the insert operation takes i milliseconds, and the kill operation takes k milliseconds. So, for example, the sequence of operations to transform algorithm into altruistic takes time $6a + d + r + 4i + k$.

(a) Show that everything to the left of the cursor is a prefix of the new string, and everything to the right of the cursor is a suffix of the old string.

(b) Devise a dynamic programming algorithm that, given two strings $x[1..n]$ and $y[1..n]$, determines the fastest time needed to transform x to y. Analyze your algorithm.

415. ☜☜ ☀ ☺☞ Suppose $A_n = \{a_1, a_2, \ldots, a_n\}$ is a set of distinct coin types, where each $a_i \in \mathbb{N}$, for $1 \le i \le n$. Suppose also that $a_1 < a_2 < \cdots < a_n$. The coin-changing problem is defined as follows. Given $C \in \mathbb{N}$, find the smallest number of coins from A_n that add up to C, given that an unlimited number of coins of each type are available. Design a dynamic programming algorithm that on inputs A_n and C, outputs the minimum number of coins needed to solve the coin-changing problem. Analyze your algorithm.

416. ☜☞ *Arbitrage* is the use of discrepancies in currency-exchange rates to make a profit. For example, there may be a small window of time during which 1 U.S. dollar buys 0.75 British pounds, 1 British pound buys 2 Australian dollars, and 1 Australian dollar buys 0.70 U.S. dollars. Then, a smart trader can trade one U.S. dollar and end up with $0.75 \times 2 \times 0.7 = 1.05$ U.S. dollars, a profit of 5%. Suppose that there are n currencies $c_1, \ldots, c_n$, and an $n \times n$ table R of exchange rates, such that one unit of currency c_i buys $R[i,j]$ units of currency c_j. Devise and analyze a dynamic programming algorithm to determine the maximum value of

$$R[c_1, c_{i_1}] \cdot R[c_{i_1}, c_{i_2}] \cdots R[c_{i_{k-1}}, c_{i_k}] \cdot R[c_{i_k}, c_1].$$

417. ☜☞ You have \$1 and want to invest it for n months. At the beginning of each month, you must choose from the following three options:

(a) Purchase a savings certificate from the local bank. Your money will be tied up for one month. If you buy it at time t, there will be a fee of $C_S(t)$ and after a month, it will return $S(t)$ for every dollar invested. That is, if you have \$$k$ at time t, then you will have \$$(k - C_S(t))S(t)$ at time $t + 1$.

(b) Purchase a state treasury bond. Your money will be tied up for six months. If you buy it at time t, there will be a fee of $C_B(t)$ and after six months, it will return $B(t)$ for every dollar invested. That is, if you have \$$k$ at time t, then you will have \$$(k - C_B(t))B(t)$ at time $t + 6$.

(c) Store the money in a sock under your mattress for a month. That is, if you have \$$k$ at time t, then you will have \$$k$ at time $t + 1$.

Suppose you have predicted values for S, B, C_S, C_B for the next n months. Devise a dynamic programming algorithm that computes the maximum amount of money that you can make over the n months in time $O(n)$.

8.6 FINDING THE SOLUTIONS

418. ☜ Show the contents of the array P for each of the parts of Problems 380–383. Write down the cheapest parenthesization of each of the matrix products.

419. ☜☞ Modify the dynamic programming algorithm for the knapsack problem so that the actual packing of the knapsack can be found. Write an algorithm for recovering the packing from the information generated by your modified dynamic programming algorithm.

420. ☜ Show the contents of the array P for each of the graphs in Problem 401. Write down the shortest path between each pair of vertices.

421. ☞☞ Modify your dynamic programming algorithm for the string-cutting problem (Problem 410) so that the cuts can be recovered. Write an algorithm for recovering the cuts from the information generated by your modified dynamic programming algorithm.

422. ☞☞ Modify your dynamic programming algorithm for the warehouse problem (Problem 412) so that the values x_i and y_i for $1 \leq i \leq n$ can be recovered. Write an algorithm for recovering these values from the information generated by your modified dynamic programming algorithm.

423. ☞☞ Modify your dynamic programming algorithm for the printing problem (Problem 413) so that the number of words on each line can be recovered. Write an algorithm for recovering these values from the information generated by your modified dynamic programming algorithm.

424. ☞☞ Modify your dynamic programming algorithm for the fastest edit-sequence problem (Problem 414) so that the fastest edit sequence can be recovered. Write an algorithm for recovering this sequence of operations from the information generated by your modified dynamic programming algorithm.

425. ☞☞ Modify your dynamic programming algorithm for the coin-changing problem (Problem 415) so that the number of each type of coin can be recovered. Write an algorithm for recovering this data from the information generated by your modified dynamic programming algorithm.

426. ☞☞ Modify your algorithm for Problem 416 to determine the sequence of currencies $i_1, i_2, \ldots, i_k$ that maximizes

$$R[c_1, c_{i_1}] \cdot R[c_{i_1}, c_{i_2}] \cdots R[i_{k-1}, i_k] \cdot R[i_k, 1].$$

427. ☞☞ Modify your algorithm for Problem 417 so that it determines the optimal investment strategy.

After graduation, you start working for a company that has a hierarchical supervisor structure in the shape of a tree, rooted at the CEO. The personnel office has ranked each employee with a conviviality rating between 0 and 10. Your first assignment is to design a dynamic programming algorithm to construct the guest list for the office Christmas party. The algorithm has input consisting of the hierarchy tree, and conviviality ratings for each employee. The output is to be a guest list that maximizes the total conviviality, and ensures that for every employee invited to the party, his or her immediate supervisor (that is, their parent in the tree) is not invited.

428. ☞☞ Design such a dynamic programming algorithm, and analyze it.

429. ☞☞ You are not sure if the CEO should get invited to the party, but you suspect that you might get fired if he is not. Can you modify your algorithm to ensure that the CEO does get invited?

8.7 HINTS

378. Start by drawing a picture of the array entries on which $m[i,j]$ depends. Make sure that the array is filled in such way that the required entries are there when they are needed.

409. Construct an array $B[1..n]$ such that $B[i]$ contains the length of the longest ascending subsequence that starts with $A[i]$, for $1 \leq i \leq n$. Fill B from back to front. From the information in B, you should be able to find the length of the longest ascending subsequence. You should also, with a little thought, be able to output a longest ascending subsequence (there may be more than one of them, obviously) in time $O(n)$.

413. In addition to the table of costs for subproblems, you will need to keep track of the number of blanks in the last line of text in the solution of each subproblem. The base case is more than just filling in the diagonal entries.

415. An $O(nC)$ time algorithm can be constructed by exploiting the similarity between the coin changing problem and the knapsack problem (see Section 8.2). It is easy to formulate an inferior algorithm that appears to run in time $O(nC^2)$, but with a little thought it can be analyzed using Harmonic numbers to give a running time of $O(C^2 \log n)$, which is superior for $C = o(n/\log n)$.

8.8 SOLUTIONS

383.

	1	2	3	4	5
1	0	48	352	1020	1096
2		0	114	792	978
3			0	684	936
4				0	2394
5					0

384. Suppose $n = 3$, and $r_0 = 1$, $r_1 = 2$, $r_2 = 32$, $r_3 = 12$. The suggested algorithm parenthesizes the product as $M_1 \cdot (M_2 \cdot M_3)$, at a cost of $2 \cdot 23 \cdot 12 + 1 \cdot 2 \cdot 12 = 792$. The most efficient way to parenthesize the product is $(M_1 \cdot M_2) \cdot M_3$, at a cost of $1 \cdot 2 \cdot 32 + 1 \cdot 32 \cdot 12 = 448$. For a larger example, take $n = 7$, and dimensions $1, 2, 32, 12, 6, 5, 17, 12$.

407. For each nonterminal symbol $S \in N$, keep a Boolean table $t_S[1..n, 1..n]$. We

will fill the tables so that for $1 \leq i \leq j \leq n$, $t_S[i,j]$ is **true** iff the string $x_i x_{i+1} \cdots x_j$ is in the language generated by S. $t_S[i,j]$ is **true** iff either $i = j$ and $S \rightarrow x_i$, or there exists k such that $i \leq k < j$ and $S \rightarrow TU$, where $t_T[i,k]$ and $t_U[k+1,j]$ are **true**.

$$\textbf{function } \text{cfl}(x_1 x_2 \cdots x_n)$$

1.   **for** each nonterminal S **do**
2.   **for** $i := 1$ **to** n **do**
3. $t_S[i,i] :=$**true** iff $S \rightarrow x_i$
4.   **for** $d := 1$ **to** $n - 1$ **do**
5.   **for** $i := 1$ **to** $n - d$ **do**
6. $j := i + d$
7.   **for** each nonterminal S **do**
8. $t_S[i,j] :=$**false**
9.   **for** each production $S \rightarrow TU$ **do**
10. $t_S[i,j] := t_S[i,j] \vee \bigvee_{k=i}^{j-1}(t_T[i,k] \wedge t_U[k+1,j])$
11.   **return**$(t_R[1,n])$ where R is the root

Since there are $O(1)$ nonterminals:

- The for-loop on lines 1–3 costs $O(n)$.
- Line 10 costs $O(n)$ (a single for-loop).
- The for-loop on lines 7–10 costs $O(n)$.
- The for-loop on lines 5–10 costs $O(n^2)$.
- The for-loop on lines 4–10 costs $O(n^3)$.

Therefore, the algorithm runs in time $O(n^3)$.

8.9 COMMENTS

380. Although the easiest way to do this is to write a program to do it for you, I recommend strongly that you do it by hand instead. It will help you to understand the subtleties of the algorithm. However, there is nothing wrong with using such a program to verify that your answer is correct.

415. In some cases, a greedy algorithm for this problem is superior to dynamic programming (see Problem 471). See also Problem 95.

Chapter 9

Greedy Algorithms

A *greedy algorithm* starts with a solution to a very small subproblem and augments it successively to a solution for the big problem. This augmentation is done in a "greedy" fashion, that is, paying attention to short-term or local gain, without regard to whether it will lead to a good long-term or global solution. As in real life, greedy algorithms sometimes lead to the best solution, sometimes lead to pretty good solutions, and sometimes lead to lousy solutions. The trick is to determine when to be greedy.

9.1 CONTINUOUS KNAPSACK

The *continuous knapsack problem* is similar to the knapsack problem studied in Section 8.2. We are given n objects, $A_1, A_2, \ldots, A_n$, where for all $1 \le i \le n$, object A_i has length s_i and weight w_i. We must fill a knapsack of length S as full as possible using fractional parts of the objects, so that the total weight is minimized, assuming that the objects are uniformly dense (so that for all $0 \le x_i \le 1$, an x_i-fraction of A_i has length $x_i s_i$ and weight $x_i w_i$). That is, we must find $0 < x_1, x_2, \ldots, x_n < 1$ that minimizes $\sum_{i=1}^{n} x_i w_i$ subject to the constraint $S = \sum_{i=1}^{n} x_i s_i$.

The greedy algorithm proceeds as follows. Define the *density* of object A_i to be w_i/s_i. Use as much of low-density objects as possible. That is, process each in increasing order of density. If the whole thing fits, use all of it. If not, fill the remaining space with a fraction of the current object, and discard the rest. That is, we first sort the objects in nondecreasing density, so that $w_i/s_i \le w_{i+1}/s_{i+1}$ for $1 \le i < n$. Then, we perform the following pseudocode:

$$s := S; \ i := 1$$
$$\textbf{while } s_i \le s \textbf{ do}$$
$$\quad x_i := 1; s := s - s_i; \ i := i + 1$$
$$x_i := s/s_i$$
$$\textbf{for } j := i + 1 \textbf{ to } n \textbf{ do } x_j := 0$$

430. ☞☞☞ 💡 📓 Show that the greedy algorithm gives a solution of minimum weight.

101

431. ☞ Solve the continuous knapsack problem on the following inputs:

    (a) $S = 20$; $s_1 = 9$, $s_2 = 5$, $s_3 = 7$, $s_4 = 12$, $s_5 = 3$; $w_1 = 4$, $w_2 = 4$, $w_3 = 8$, $w_4 = 5$, $w_5 = 1$.

    (b) $S = 18$; $s_1 = 9$, $s_2 = 5$, $s_3 = 7$, $s_4 = 12$, $s_5 = 3$; $w_1 = 18$, $w_2 = 15$, $w_3 = 28$, $w_4 = 50$, $w_5 = 6$.

    (c) $S = 25$; $s_1 = 12$, $s_2 = 6$, $s_3 = 17$, $s_4 = 32$, $s_5 = 23$; $w_1 = 18$, $w_2 = 15$, $w_3 = 28$, $w_4 = 50$, $w_5 = 47$.

9.2 DIJKSTRA'S ALGORITHM

The *single-source shortest-paths* problem is defined as follows. Given a labeled, directed graph $G = (V, E)$ and a distinguished vertex $s \in V$, find for each vertex $w \in V$, the shortest (that is, least-cost) path from s to w. (See also Problem 367 for the unweighted version of this problem, that is, all edge labels are equal to unity.) Vertex s is called the *source*.

    Dijkstra's algorithm for the single-source shortest-paths problem is the following. $C[i, j]$ denotes the cost of the edge from vertex i to vertex j.

    1. $S := \{s\}$
    2.   **for** each $v \in V$ **do**
    3. $D[v] := C[s, v]$
    4.   **if** $(s, v) \in E$ **then** $P[v] := s$ **else** $P[v] := 0$
    5.   **for** $i := 1$ **to** $n - 1$ **do**
    6.   choose $w \in V - S$ with smallest $D[w]$
    7. $S := S \cup \{w\}$
    8.   **for** each vertex $v \in V$ **do**
    9.   **if** $D[w] + C[w, v] < D[v]$ **then**
    10. $D[v] := D[w] + C[w, v]$; $P[v] := w$

432. ☞ Show the contents of arrays D and P after each iteration of the main for-loop in Dijkstra's algorithm executed on the graphs shown in Figure 9.1, with source vertex 1. Use this information to list the shortest paths from vertex 1 to each of the other vertices.

433. ☞☞ Show that an arbitrary collection of single-source shortest paths in an undirected graph does not necessarily form a spanning tree.

434. ☞☞ Show that the single-source shortest paths constructed by Dijkstra's algorithm on a connected undirected graph form a spanning tree. (See also Problem 433.)

435. ☞☞ Is the spanning tree formed by Dijkstra's algorithm on a connected undirected graph a min-cost spanning tree? (See also Problem 434.)

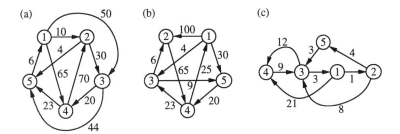

Figure 9.1. Some graphs.

436. 🎓 🎓 ☺︎ Suppose we want to solve the single-source *longest* path problem. Can we modify Dijkstra's algorithm to solve this problem by changing *minimum* to *maximum*? If so, then prove your algorithm correct. If not, then provide a counterexample.

437. 🎓 🎓 Suppose you are the programmer for a travel agent trying to determine the minimum *elapsed time* from DFW airport to cities all over the world. Since you got an A in my algorithms course, you immediately think of using Dijkstra's algorithm on the graph of cities, with an edge between two cities labeled with the flying time between them. But the shortest path in this graph corresponds to shortest flying time, which does not include the time spent waiting at various airports for connecting flights. Desperate, you instead label each edge from city x to city y with a function $f_{xy}(t)$ that maps from your arrival time at x to your arrival time at y in the following fashion: If you are in x at time t, then you will be in y at time $f_{xy}(t)$ (including waiting time and flying time). Modify Dijkstra's algorithm to work under this new formulation, and explain why it works. State clearly any assumptions that you make (for example, it is reasonable to assume that $f_{xy}(t) \geq t$).

9.3 MIN-COST SPANNING TREES

A graph $S = (V, T)$ is a *spanning tree* of an undirected graph $G = (V, E)$ if S is a tree (that is, S is connected and has no cycles), and $T \subseteq E$. It is a *min-cost spanning tree* of a labeled graph if it is a spanning tree of smallest cost.

Prim's algorithm constructs a spanning tree using a priority queue Q of edges, as follows:

1. $T := \emptyset$; $V_1 := \{1\}$; $Q := \text{empty}$
2.   **for** each $w \in V$ such that $(1, w) \in E$ **do**
3.   insert$(Q, (1, w))$
4.   **while** $|V_1| < n$ **do**
5. $e :=$ deletemin(Q)
6.   Suppose $e = (u, v)$, where $u \in V_1$
7.   **if** $v \notin V_1$ **then**
8. $T := T \cup \{e\}$
9. $V_1 := V_1 \cup \{v\}$
10.   **for** each $w \in V$ such that $(v, w) \in E$ **do**
11.   insert$(Q, (v, w))$

Kruskal's algorithm constructs a spanning tree using the union-find abstract data type (see Section 11.4). F is the set of vertex-sets in the forest.

1. $T := \emptyset$; $F := \emptyset$
2.   **for** each vertex $v \in V$ **do** $F := F \cup \{\{v\}\}$
3.   Sort edges in E in ascending order of cost
4.   **while** $|F| > 1$ **do**
5. $(u, v) :=$ the next edge in sorted order
6.   **if** find$(u) \neq$ find(v) **then**
7.   union(u, v)
8. $T := T \cup \{(u, v)\}$

438.   ☞ Draw the spanning forest after every iteration of the main while-loop in Kruskal's algorithm on each of the graphs in Figure 9.1, ignoring the directions on the edges.

439.   ☞ Draw the spanning forest after every iteration of the main while-loop in Prim's algorithm on each of the graphs in Figure 9.1, ignoring the directions on the edges.

440.   ☞ Draw the spanning forest after every iteration of the main while-loop in Kruskal's algorithm on the graph shown in Figure 9.2. Number the edges in order of selection.

441.   ☞ Draw the spanning forest after every iteration of the main while-loop in Prim's algorithm on the graph shown in Figure 9.2. Number the edges in order of selection.

442.   ☞ Would Prim's algorithm start by making the choice of edges shown in Figure 9.4 for the graph shown in Figure 9.3?

443.   ☞ Would Kruskal's algorithm start by making the choice of edges shown in Figure 9.5 on the graph shown in Figure 9.3?

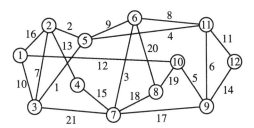

Figure 9.2. A graph.

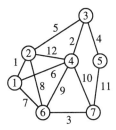

Figure 9.3. Another graph.

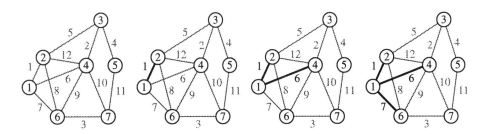

Figure 9.4. A min-cost spanning tree under construction using Prim's algorithm?

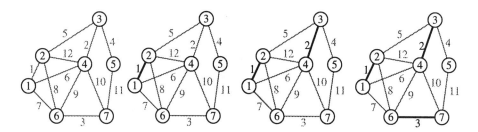

Figure 9.5. A min-cost spanning tree under construction using Kruskal's algorithm?

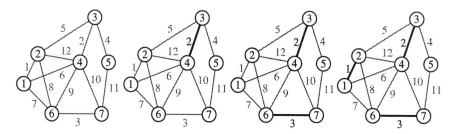

Figure 9.6. A min-cost spanning tree under construction?

444. ☞ Could a greedy algorithm for min-cost spanning trees start by making the choice of edges shown in Figure 9.6 on the graph shown in Figure 9.3?

445. ☞ Could a greedy algorithm for min-cost spanning trees start by making the choice of edges shown in Figure 9.7 on the graph shown in Figure 9.3?

446. ☞ ☞ ۞ Show that Prim's algorithm and Kruskal's algorithm always construct the same min-cost spanning tree on a connected undirected graph in which the edge costs are distinct.

447. ☞ ☞ ۞ Show that Prim's algorithm and Kruskal's algorithm always construct the same min-cost spanning tree on a connected undirected graph in which no pair of edges that share a vertex have the same cost.

448. ☞ ☞ Is the path between a pair of vertices in a min-cost spanning tree of an undirected graph necessarily a min-cost path? Is this true if the min-cost spanning tree is unique? If it is not unique?

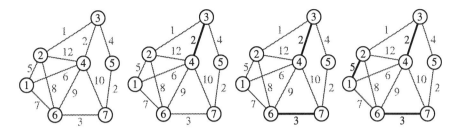

Figure 9.7. A min-cost spanning tree under construction?

449. 🎓🎓 💡 Show how to modify Prim's algorithm so that it runs in time $O(n \log k)$ on a graph that has only k different edge costs.

450. 🎓🎓 Here is a version of Prim's algorithm that is different from the one given earlier in this section. Is it correct? If so, prove it correct. If not, explain why it is wrong and give a graph on which it fails.

$$
\begin{aligned}
&1. \quad T := \emptyset;\ V_1 := \{1\};\ Q := \text{empty}\\
&2. \quad \textbf{for } \text{each } w \in V \text{ such that } (1, w) \in E \textbf{ do}\\
&3 \qquad \text{insert}(Q, (1, w))\\
&4. \quad \textbf{while } |V_1| < n \textbf{ do}\\
&5. \qquad e := \text{deletemin}(Q)\\
&6. \qquad \text{Suppose } e = (u, v),\ \text{where } u \in V_1\\
&7. \qquad T := T \cup \{e\}\\
&8. \qquad V_1 := V_1 \cup \{v\}\\
&9. \qquad \textbf{for } \text{each } w \in V \text{ such that } (v, w) \in E \textbf{ do}\\
&10. \qquad\quad \textbf{if } w \notin V_1 \textbf{ then } \text{insert}(Q, (v, w))
\end{aligned}
$$

In the vanilla version of Prim's algorithm and Kruskal's algorithm, it is not specified what to do if a choice must be made between two edges of minimum cost.

451. 🎓 Prove that for Prim's algorithm, it doesn't matter which of the two edges is chosen.

452. 🎓 Prove that for Kruskal's algorithm, it doesn't matter which of the two edges is chosen.

453. 🎓 Suppose that there are exactly two edges that have the same cost. Does Prim's algorithm construct the same min-cost spanning tree regardless of which edge is chosen?

454. ☞ Suppose that there are exactly two edges that have the same cost. Does Kruskal's algorithm construct the same min-cost spanning tree regardless of which edge is chosen?

455. ☞☞ Suppose Prim's algorithm and Kruskal's algorithm choose the lexicographically first edge first. That is, if a choice must be made between two distinct edges, $e_1 = (u_1, v_1)$ and $e_2 = (u_2, v_2)$ of the same cost, where $u_1 < v_1$ and $u_2 < v_2$, then the following strategy is used. Suppose the vertices are numbered $1, 2, \ldots, n$. Choose e_1 if $u_1 < u_2$, or $u_1 = u_2$ and $v_1 < v_2$. Otherwise, choose e_2. Prove that under these conditions, both algorithms construct the same min-cost spanning tree.

456. ☞☞ Design an algorithm for the *max-cost* spanning tree.

A *directed spanning tree* of a directed graph is a spanning tree in which the directions on the edges point from parent to child.

457. ☞☞ Suppose Prim's algorithm is modified to take the cheapest edge directed *out* of the tree.

    (a) Does it find a directed spanning tree of a directed graph?
    (b) If so, will it find a directed spanning tree of minimum cost?

458. ☞☞ Suppose Kruskal's algorithm is used to construct a directed spanning tree.

    (a) Does it find a directed spanning tree of a directed graph?
    (b) If so, will it find a directed spanning tree of minimum cost?

459. ☞☞ Consider the following algorithm. Suppose Prim's algorithm is modified as described in Problem 457, and then run n times, starting at each vertex in turn. The output is the cheapest of the n directed spanning trees.

    (a) Does this algorithm output a directed spanning tree of a directed graph?
    (b) If so, will it find a directed spanning tree of minimum cost?

Consider the following algorithm for finding a min-cost spanning tree. Suppose the graph has vertices numbered $1, 2, \ldots, n$. Start with a forest containing n trees, each consisting of a single vertex. Repeat the following until a single tree remains. For each vertex $v = 1, 2, \ldots, n$ in turn, consider the cheapest edge with at least one endpoint in the tree that contains v. If it has both endpoints in the same tree, then discard it. If not, then add it to the spanning forest.

460. ☞☞ Is this algorithm correct? Justify your answer.

461. ☞☞ Explain how to implement this algorithm in time $O(e \log n)$.

9.4   TRAVELING SALESPERSON

The *traveling salesperson* problem is defined as follows. Given a directed labeled graph, find a Hamiltonian cycle of minimum total cost. A "vanilla" greedy algorithm for the traveling salesperson problem starts at node number 1, and moves along the edge of minimum cost to the next node, and repeats this until it finds a node that it has visited before, or can go no further.

462. ☞ Show that this greedy algorithm may fail to find a cycle.

463. ☞ Show that even when the greedy algorithm finds a cycle, it may not be a Hamiltonian cycle, even when one exists in the graph.

464. ☞☞ Suppose the greedy algorithm does find a Hamiltonian cycle. Prove that it is a Hamiltonian cycle of minimum cost.

465. ☞☞ Suppose the edge costs are distinct, and the greedy algorithm does find a Hamiltonian cycle. Show that it is the only min-cost Hamiltonian cycle in the graph.

466. ☞☞ Here is another greedy algorithm for the traveling salesperson problem. Simply run the vanilla greedy algorithm described above n times, starting at each vertex in turn, and output the cheapest Hamiltonian cycle found. Suppose this greedy algorithm does output a Hamiltonian cycle. Can it be a different cycle from the one found by the vanilla greedy algorithm? Justify your answer.

Another greedy algorithm for the traveling salesperson problem proceeds as follows. Start at node number 1, and move along the edge of minimum cost that leads to an unvisited node, repeating this until the algorithm arrives at a vertex from which all edges lead to visited nodes.

467. ☞ Show that this greedy algorithm may fail to find a cycle.

468. ☞ Suppose the graph has a Hamiltonian cycle. Will this algorithm find it?

469. ☞☞ Suppose this greedy algorithm finds a Hamiltonian cycle. Is it necessarily a Hamiltonian cycle of minimum cost? Justify your answer.

9.5   APPLICATIONS

The problems in this section ask you to apply the greedy method in new situations. One thing you will notice about greedy algorithms is that they are usually easy to design, easy to implement, easy to analyze, and they are very fast, but they are almost always difficult to prove correct.

470. ☞ ☞ 📐 Given n files of length $m_1, m_2, \ldots, m_n$, the *optimal tape-storage problem* is to find which order is the best to store them on a tape, assuming that each retrieval starts with the tape rewound, each retrieval takes time equal to the length of the preceding files in the tape plus the length of the retrieved file, and that files are to be retrieved in the reverse order. The greedy algorithm puts the files on the tape in ascending order of size. Prove that this is the best order.

471. ☞ ☞ 💡 ☺☞ Suppose $A_n = \{a_1, a_2, \ldots, a_n\}$ is a set of distinct coin types, where each $a_i \in \mathbb{N}$, for $1 \leq i \leq n$. Suppose also that $a_1 < a_2 < \cdots < a_n$. The coin-changing problem is defined as follows. Given $C \in \mathbb{N}$, find the smallest number of coins from A_n that add up to C, given that an unlimited number of coins of each type are available.

    (a) Suppose $a_1 = 1$. A greedy algorithm will make change by using the larger coins first, using as many coins of each type as it can before it moves to the next lower denomination. Show that this algorithm does not necessarily generate a solution with the minimum number of coins.

    (b) Show that for all $c \in \mathbb{N}$, if $A_n = \{1, c, c^2, \ldots, c^{n-1}\}$, $c \geq 2$, then for all $C \in \mathbb{N}$, the greedy algorithm always gives a minimal solution to the coin-changing problem.

472. ☞ ☞ The *vertex cover problem* is defined as follows. Let $G = (V, E)$ be an undirected graph. A *vertex cover* of G is a set $U \subseteq V$ such that for each edge $(u, v) \in E$, either $u \in U$ or $v \in U$. A *minimum vertex cover* is a vertex cover with the smallest number of vertices in it. The following is a greedy algorithm for this problem:

            function cover(V, E)
    1. $U := \emptyset$
    2.   **repeat**
    3.   let $v \in V$ be a vertex of maximum degree
    4. $U := U \cup \{v\}; V := V - \{v\}$
    5. $E := E - \{(u, w)$ such that $u = v$ or $w = v\}$
    6.   **until** $E = \emptyset$
    7.   **return**(U)

Does this algorithm always generate a minimum vertex cover? Justify your answer.

473. ☞ ☞ The *one-processor scheduling problem* is defined as follows. We are given a set of n jobs. Each job i has a start time t_i, and a deadline d_i. A *feasible schedule* is a permutation of the jobs such that when the jobs are performed in that order, then every job is finished before the deadline. A greedy algorithm for the one-processor scheduling problem processes the jobs

in order of deadline (the early deadlines before the late ones). Show that if a feasible schedule exists, then the schedule produced by this greedy algorithm is feasible.

9.6 HINTS

430. Show that a greedy solution $(x_1, x_2, \ldots, x_n)$ can be changed to an optimal solution $(y_1, y_2, \ldots, y_n)$ without affecting its length by doing the following for $i = 1, 2, \ldots, n$. Change x_i to y_i and adjust the remaining $x_{i+1}, \ldots, x_n$ so that the length remains the same.

446. This can be proved directly by induction. But a more insightful way to do it is to prove that the min-cost spanning tree is unique under these conditions.

447. See Problem 446.

449. This is really a data structures question.

471. For part (a), just play around until you get a counterexample. For part (b), show that there is only one solution in which the number of coins of each type is less than c, and that the min-cost solution must have this form. These two facts should enable you to easily prove that the greedy algorithm does the right thing.

9.7 SOLUTIONS

430. Let $X = (x_1, x_2, \ldots, x_n)$ be the solution generated by the greedy algorithm. If all the x_i are 1, then the solution is clearly optimal (it is the only solution). Otherwise, let j be the smallest number such that $x_j \neq 1$. From the algorithm,

$$x_i = 1 \quad \text{for} \quad 1 \leq i < j$$
$$0 \leq x_j < 1$$
$$x_i = 0 \quad \text{for} \quad j < i \leq n.$$

Therefore,

$$\sum_{i=1}^{j} x_i s_i = S. \tag{9.1}$$

Let $Y = (y_1, y_2, \ldots, y_n)$ be a solution of minimal weight. We will prove that X must have the same weight as Y, and hence has minimal weight too. If $X = Y$, we are done. Otherwise, let k be the least number such that $x_k \neq y_k$.

It must be the case that $y_k < x_k$. To see this, consider the three possible cases:

Case 1. $k < j$. Then $x_k = 1$. Therefore, since $x_k \neq y_k$, y_k must be smaller than x_k.

Case 2. $k = j$. By the definition of k, $x_k \neq y_k$. If $y_k > x_k$,

$$
\begin{aligned}
\sum_{i=1}^{n} y_i s_i &= \sum_{i=1}^{k-1} y_i s_i + y_k s_k + \sum_{i=k+1}^{n} y_i s_i \\
&= \sum_{i=1}^{k-1} x_i s_i + y_k s_k + \sum_{i=k+1}^{n} y_i s_i \\
&= S + (y_k - x_k)s_k + \sum_{i=k+1}^{n} y_i s_i \text{ (by Equation 9.1, since } k = j) \\
&> S,
\end{aligned}
$$

which contradicts the fact that Y is a solution. Therefore, $y_k < x_k$.

Case 3. $k > j$. Then $x_k = 0$ and $y_k > 0$, and so

$$
\begin{aligned}
\sum_{i=1}^{n} y_i s_i &= \sum_{i=1}^{j} y_i s_i + \sum_{i=j+1}^{n} y_i s_i \\
&= \sum_{i=1}^{j} x_i s_i + \sum_{i=j+1}^{n} y_i s_i \\
&= S + \sum_{i=j+1}^{n} y_i s_i \text{ (by Equation 9.1)} \\
&> S.
\end{aligned}
$$

This is not possible, hence Case 3 can never happen. In the other two cases, $y_k < x_k$ as claimed. Now that we have established that $y_k < x_k$, we can return to the proof. Suppose we increase y_k to x_k, and decrease as many of $y_{k+1}, \ldots, y_n$ as necessary to make the total length remain at S. Call this new solution $Z = (z_1, z_2, \ldots, z_n)$. Then,

$$(z_k - y_k)s_k > 0, \tag{9.2}$$

$$\sum_{i=k+1}^{n} (z_i - y_i)s_i < 0, \tag{9.3}$$

$$(z_k - y_k)s_k + \sum_{i=k+1}^{n} (z_i - y_i)s_i = 0. \tag{9.4}$$

Therefore,

$$
\begin{aligned}
\sum_{i=1}^{n} z_i w_i \;=\;& \sum_{i=1}^{k-1} z_i w_i + z_k w_k + \sum_{i=k+1}^{n} z_i w_i \\[2mm]
=\;& \sum_{i=1}^{k-1} y_i w_i + z_k w_k + \sum_{i=k+1}^{n} z_i w_i \\[2mm]
=\;& \sum_{i=1}^{n} y_i w_i - y_k w_k - \sum_{i=k+1}^{n} y_i w_i + z_k w_k + \sum_{i=k+1}^{n} z_i w_i \\[2mm]
=\;& \sum_{i=1}^{n} y_i w_i + (z_k - y_k) w_k + \sum_{i=k+1}^{n} (z_i - y_i) w_i \\[2mm]
=\;& \sum_{i=1}^{n} y_i w_i + (z_k - y_k) s_k w_k / s_k + \sum_{i=k+1}^{n} (z_i - y_i) s_i w_i / s_i \\[2mm]
\leq\;& \sum_{i=1}^{n} y_i w_i + (z_k - y_k) s_k w_k / s_k + \sum_{i=k+1}^{n} (z_i - y_i) s_i w_k / s_k
\end{aligned}
$$

(by Equation 9.4 and density)

$$
\begin{aligned}
=\;& \sum_{i=1}^{n} y_i w_i + \left((z_k - y_k) s_k + \sum_{i=k+1}^{n} (z_i - y_i) s_i \right) w_k / s_k \\[2mm]
=\;& \sum_{i=1}^{n} y_i w_i \quad \text{(by Equation 9.4).}
\end{aligned}
$$

Now, since Y is a minimal-weight solution,

$$
\sum_{i=1}^{n} z_i w_i \not< \sum_{i=1}^{n} y_i w_i.
$$

Hence, Y and Z have the same weight. But Z looks "more like" X than Y does, in the sense that the first k entries of Z are the same as X, whereas only the first $k-1$ entries of Y are the same as X. Repeating this procedure sufficiently often transforms Y into X and maintains the same weight. Therefore, X must have minimal weight.

470. Suppose we have files $f_1, f_2, \ldots, f_n$, of lengths $m_1, m_2, \ldots, m_n$, respectively. Let $i_1, i_2, \ldots, i_n$ be a permutation of $1, 2, \ldots, n$. Suppose we store the files in order

$$
f_{i_1}, f_{i_2}, \ldots, f_{i_n}.
$$

To retrieve the kth file on the tape, f_{i_k}, costs $\sum_{j=1}^{k} m_{i_j}$. Therefore, the cost of retrieving them all is

$$\sum_{k=1}^{n} \sum_{j=1}^{k} m_{i_j} = \sum_{k=1}^{n} (n-k+1)m_{i_k}. \tag{9.5}$$

To see this, consider the following table of costs:

$$
\begin{aligned}
f_{i_1}: &\quad m_{i_1} \\
f_{i_2}: &\quad m_{i_1}+m_{i_2} \\
f_{i_3}: &\quad m_{i_1}+m_{i_2}+m_{i_3} \\
&\quad \vdots \\
f_{i_{n-1}}: &\quad m_{i_1}+m_{i_2}+m_{i_3}+\cdots+m_{i_{n-1}} \\
f_{i_n}: &\quad m_{i_1}+m_{i_2}+m_{i_3}+\cdots+m_{i_{n-1}}+m_{i_n}
\end{aligned}
$$

The left-hand side of Equation 9.5 adds this table by rows. If the total is computed by columns, we get instead

$$nm_{i_1} + (n-1)m_{i_2} + (n-2)m_{i_3} + \cdots + 2m_{i_{n-1}} + m_{i_n} = \sum_{k=1}^{n} (n-k+1)m_{i_k},$$

which is the right-hand side of Equation (9.5). The greedy algorithm picks files f_i in nondecreasing order of their size m_i. It remains to prove that this is the minimum cost permutation.

Claim: Any permutation in nondecreasing order of m_i's has minimum cost.
Proof: Let $\Pi = (i_1, i_2, \ldots, i_n)$ be a permutation of $1, 2, \ldots, n$ that is not in nondecreasing order of m_i's. We will prove that it cannot have minimum cost. Since $m_{i_1}, m_{i_2}, \ldots, m_{i_n}$ is not in nondecreasing order, there must exist $1 \le j < n$ such that $m_{i_j} > m_{i_{j+1}}$. Let Π' be permutation Π with i_j and i_{j+1} swapped. The cost of permutation Π is

$$
\begin{aligned}
C(\Pi) &= \sum_{k=1}^{n} (n-k+1)m_{i_k} \\
&= \sum_{k=1}^{j-1} (n-k+1)m_{i_k} + (n-j+1)m_{i_j} + (n-j)m_{i_{j+1}} \\
&\quad + \sum_{k=j+2}^{n} (n-k+1)m_{i_k}.
\end{aligned}
$$

The cost of permutation Π' is

$$C(\Pi') = \sum_{k=1}^{j-1} (n-k+1)m_{i_k} + (n-j+1)m_{i_{j+1}} + (n-j)m_{i_j} + \sum_{k=j+2}^{n} (n-k+1)m_{i_k}.$$

Hence,

$$
\begin{aligned}
C(\Pi) - C(\Pi') &= (n - j + 1)(m_{i_j} - m_{i_{j+1}}) + (n - j)(m_{i_{j+1}} - m_{i_j}) \\
&= m_{i_j} - m_{i_{j+1}} \\
&> 0 \quad \text{(by definition of } j\text{)}.
\end{aligned}
$$

Therefore, $C(\Pi') < C(\Pi)$, and so Π cannot be a permutation of minimum cost. This is true of any Π that is not in nondecreasing order of m_i's. Therefore, the minimum-cost permutation must be in nondecreasing order of m_i's.

9.8   COMMENTS

436, 456. These problems were suggested to the author by Farhad Shahrokhi in 1993.

471. See also Problem 95. In general, a dynamic programming algorithm is the best solution to this problem (see Problem 415). This question is designed to illustrate the point that a greedy algorithm is better in some (but not all) cases.

Chapter 10

Exhaustive Search

Often it appears that there is no better way to solve a problem than to try all possible solutions. This approach, called *exhaustive search*, is almost always slow, but sometimes it is better than nothing. It may actually be practical in real situations if the problem size is small enough. The most commonly used algorithmic technique used in exhaustive search is divide-and-conquer (see Chapter 7).

The approach taken to exhaustive search in this chapter is very different from that taken by most textbooks. Most exhaustive search problems can be reduced to the problem of generating simple combinatorial objects, most often strings, permutations, and combinations. Sections 10.1–10.4 cover some simple algorithms that form our basic tools. Section 10.6 covers the application of these tools to various interesting exhaustive search problems. Section 10.5 compares exhaustive search algorithms to backtracking. Sometimes backtracking is faster, sometimes not.

10.1 STRINGS

A bit-string is an array of n bits. Bit-strings are often used to represent sets (the term usually used is the *bit-vector* representation of a set). The following is a recursive algorithm for generating bit-strings. We assume the existence of a procedure process(C) that processes a bit-string stored in an array C. Our aim is to process all bit-strings of a fixed length.

> **procedure** binary(m)
> **comment** process all binary strings of length m
> 1. **if** $m = 0$ **then** process(C) **else**
> 2. $C[m] := 0$; binary($m - 1$)
> 3. $C[m] := 1$; binary($m - 1$)

474. ☞ Show that the algorithm is correct, that is, that a call to binary(n) processes all binary strings of length n.

475. ☞ How many assignments to array C are made (that is, how often are lines 2 and 3 executed)? Hence, deduce the running time of the procedure.

The following algorithm generates all strings of n bits in an array $C[1..n]$. A sentinel is used at both ends of C, so C is actually an array indexed from 0 to $n+1$. The operation "complement a bit" used in line 8 means change it from a 0 to a 1, or vice-versa. It works by treating C as a binary number and repeatedly incrementing it through all 2^n possible values.

1. **for** $i := 0$ **to** $n+1$ **do** $C[i] := 0$
2. **while** $C[n+1] = 0$ **do**
3.   process(C)
4.   increment(C)

    procedure increment(C)
5. $i := 1$
6.   **while** $C[i-1] = 0$ **do**
7.   Complement $C[i]$
8. $i := i+1$

476. ☞ Prove that the algorithm is correct, that is, that procedure process(C) is called once with $C[1..n]$ containing each string of n bits.

477. ☞ Prove that for all $n \geq 1$, the number of times that a bit of C is complemented (that is, the number of times that line 7 is executed) is $2^{n+1} - (n+2)$. Hence, deduce the running time of the algorithm.

A *minimal-change* algorithm for generating bit-strings generates them in such an order that each string differs from its predecessor in exactly one place. The following algorithm generates all of the bit-strings of length n in minimal-change order. The array b is initially set to all zeros, and the bit-strings are generated with a call to generate(n).

    procedure generate(n)
1.   **if** $n = 0$ **then** process(b)
2.   **else**
3.   generate($n-1$)
4.   Complement $b[n]$
5.   generate($n-1$)

478. ☞ ☺☞ Prove that this algorithm does generate the 2^n bit-strings of length n in minimal-change order.

479. ☞ Prove that for all $n \geq 1$, the number of times that a bit of b is complemented (that is, the number of times that line 4 is executed) is $2^n - 1$. Hence, deduce the running time of the algorithm.

A *k-ary string* is a string of digits drawn from $\{0, 1, \ldots, k-1\}$. For example, if $k = 2$, then a k-ary string is simply a binary string.

480. ☞ Design an optimal exhaustive search algorithm for generating all k-ary strings of length n in lexicographic order in time $O(k^n)$. For example, if $k = 3$ and $n = 4$, then your algorithm should generate the strings

$$0000, 0001, 0002, 0010, 0011, 0012, 0020, 0021, 0022, 0100, \ldots, 2221, 2222.$$

481. ☞ Prove that your algorithm for Problem 480 is correct.

482. ☞ Analyze the running time of your algorithm for Problem 480.

A *minimal-change* algorithm for generating k-ary strings generates them in such an order that each string differs from its predecessor in exactly one place.

483. ☞ ☞ Design a minimal-change exhaustive search algorithm for generating all k-ary strings of length n. (See also Problem 480.)

484. ☞ Prove that your algorithm for Problem 483 is correct.

485. ☞ Analyze the running time of your algorithm for Problem 483.

10.2 PERMUTATIONS

Consider the problem of exhaustively generating all permutations of n things. Suppose $A[1..n]$ contains n distinct values. The following algorithm generates all permutations of $A[1..n]$ in the following sense: A call to procedure permute(n) will result in procedure process(A) being called once with $A[1..n]$ containing each permutation of its contents.

> **procedure** permute(n)
> 1.   **if** $n = 1$ **then** process(A) **else**
> 2. $B := A$
> 3.   permute($n - 1$)
> 4.   **for** $i := 1$ **to** $n - 1$ **do**
> 5.   swap $A[n]$ with $A[1]$
> 6.   permute($n - 1$)
> 7. $A := B$ cyclically shifted one place right

486. ☞ ☞ Prove that this algorithm calls process(A) with A containing each permutation of n entries exactly once.

487. ☞☞ ☀ ☞ What is the running time of this algorithm?

488. ☞☞☞ Show that the effect of line 7 is the same as performing a cyclic shift of $A[2..n]$. Use this observation to eliminate the need for the array B. Does this affect the running time of the algorithm?

Consider the following algorithm for generating all permutations. To generate all permutations of any n distinct values in $A[1..n]$, call permute(1).

> **procedure** permute(i)
> 1.   **if** $i = n$ **then** process(A) **else**
> 4.   permute($i + 1$)
> 2.   **for** $j := i + 1$ **to** n **do**
> 3.   swap $A[i]$ with $A[j]$
> 4.   permute($i + 1$)
> 5.   swap $A[i]$ with $A[j]$

489. ☞☞ Prove this algorithm correct.

490. ☞ How many swaps are made by this algorithm, as a function of n? What is its running time?

The following is a *minimal-change* algorithm for generating permutations. That is, each permutation generated differs from the previous one by having just two values swapped. It is known as *Heap's algorithm* (Heap [35]).

> **procedure** permute(n)
> 1.   **for** $i := 1$ **to** n **do** $A[i] := i$
> 2.   **if** n is odd
> 3.   **then** oddpermute(n)
> 4.   **else** evenpermute(n)
>
> **procedure** oddpermute(n)
> 5.   **if** $n = 1$ **then** process **else**
> 6.   evenpermute($n - 1$)
> 7.   **for** $i := 1$ **to** $n - 1$ **do**
> 8.   swap $A[1]$ and $A[n]$
> 9.   evenpermute($n - 1$)
>
> **procedure** evenpermute(n)
> 10.   **if** $n = 1$ **then** process **else**
> 11.   oddpermute($n - 1$)
> 12.   **for** $i := 1$ **to** $n - 1$ **do**
> 13.   swap $A[i]$ and $A[n]$
> 14.   oddpermute($n - 1$)

491. 🎓🎓🎓 💡 Show that the algorithm is correct, that is, it generates all permutations in minimal-change order.

492. 🎓🎓 Show that Heap's algorithm uses the minimum number of swaps, (that is, $n! - 1$ swaps). What is its running time?

10.3   COMBINATIONS

Consider the problem of generating all combinations of r things chosen from n, for some $0 \leq r \leq n$. We will, without loss of generality, assume that the n items to be chosen from are the natural numbers $1, 2, \ldots, n$.

The following algorithm generates all combinations of r things drawn from n in the following sense: Procedure process(A) is called once with $A[1..r]$ containing each combination. To use it, call procedure choose($1, r$).

> **procedure** choose(b, c)
> **comment** choose c elements out of $b..n$
> 1.   **if** $c = 0$ **then** process(A)
> 2.   **else for** $i := b$ **to** $n - c + 1$ **do**
> 3. $A[c] := i$
> 4.   choose($i + 1, c - 1$)

493. 🎓🎓 Prove that this algorithm is correct.

494. 🎓 Prove that the combinations generated by this algorithm are in descending order, that is, when process(A) is called, $A[i] > A[i + 1]$ for all $1 \leq i < n$.

495. 🎓🎓 Let $T(n, r)$ be the number of assignments to array A. Show that $T(n, r) \leq r \binom{n}{r}$. Hence, deduce that the algorithm runs in time $O\left(r \binom{n}{r}\right)$.

496. 🎓🎓 Show that for all $1 \leq r \leq n/2$, $T(n, r) \leq 2 \binom{n}{r} - r$. Hence, deduce that the algorithm is optimal for $r \leq n/2$.

A *minimal-change* algorithm for combinations generates them in such a manner that each choice of r objects differs from the previous one by having one object removed and replaced by another. The following is a minimal-change algorithm for generating combinations. It is used by calling up($1, r$).

procedure up(b, c)
1.   **if** $c = 0$ **then** process(a)
2.   **else for** $i := b$ **to** n **do**
3. $a[r - c + 1] := i$
4.   **if** i is odd **then** up$(i + 1, c - 1)$ **else** down$(i + 1, c - 1)$

procedure down(b, c)
5.   **if** $c = 0$ **then** process(a)
6.   **else for** $i := n$ **downto** b **do**
7. $a[r - c + 1] := i$
8.   **if** i is odd **then** up$(i + 1, c - 1)$ **else** down$(i + 1, c - 1)$

497. ☞☞ ☺☞ Prove that the algorithm is correct, that is, that procedure process(a) is called with a containing a sequence of combinations in minimal-change order.

498. ☞ How many assignments to a does the algorithm make? Hence, deduce its running time.

499. ☞ Prove that the combinations generated by this algorithm are in ascending order, that is, when process(a) is called, $a[i] < a[i + 1]$ for all $1 \le i < n$.

10.4   OTHER ELEMENTARY ALGORITHMS

If n is even, a *perfect matching* of size n is an unordered sequence of unordered pairs $(v_1, v_2), (v_3, v_4), \ldots, (v_{n-1}, v_n)$, where $\{v_1, v_2, \ldots, v_n\} = \{1, 2, \ldots, n\}$. Note that two perfect matchings are deemed to be identical even if the pairs are listed in a different order, and the values within each pair are listed in a different order. The following is an algorithm for generating all perfect matchings of size n in an array $M[1..n]$, where n is even:

procedure match(n)
1.   **if** $n = 2$ **then** process(M) **else**
2.   match$(n - 2)$
3.   **for** $i := n - 2$ **downto** 1 **do**
4.   swap $A[i]$ with $A[n - 1]$
5.   match$(n - 2)$
6.   circular shift $A[1..n - 1]$ one place right

500. ☞ Let $M(n)$ be the number of perfect matchings of n values. Show that if n is even, then

$$M(n) = \prod_{i=1}^{n/2} (2i - 1).$$

501. 🎓🎓 Prove that the algorithm is correct.

502. 🎓🎓 💡 Show that the algorithm runs in time $O(M(n))$.

503. 🎓 If n is odd, the definition of perfect matching is similar except that there is a leftover value that is not paired with any other. What is $M(n)$ when n is odd? How can the above algorithm be used to generate all perfect matchings when n is odd, in time $O(M(n))$?

Suppose you have m marbles and n jars, each of which can hold at most c marbles.

504. 🎓🎓 Use divide-and-conquer to design an algorithm that generates all of the ways of distributing the marbles into the jars so that no jar holds more than c marbles, where $m \leq cn$. Your algorithm must print the number of marbles in each jar for each of the different ways of distributing the marbles. So, for example, with $m = 10$, $n = 3$, and $c = 5$, the output of your algorithm would be

0	5	5	3	2	5	4	3	3	5	3	2
1	4	5	3	3	4	4	4	2	5	4	1
1	5	4	3	4	3	4	5	1	5	5	0
2	3	5	3	5	2	5	0	5			
2	4	4	4	1	5	5	1	4			
2	5	3	4	2	4	5	2	3			

505. 🎓 Prove that your algorithm for Problem 504 is correct.

506. 🎓 Analyze the running time of your algorithm for Problem 504.

10.5   BACKTRACKING

Backtracking is a type of exhaustive search in which the combinatorial object is constructed recursively, and the recursion tree is *pruned*, that is, recursive calls are not made when the part of the current object that has already been constructed cannot lead to a valid or optimal solution. For example, the recursive algorithm for generating bit-strings from Section 10.1 can be modified easily to give a backtracking algorithm for generating all bit-strings of length n with k or fewer bits. To use the algorithm, call binary$(n, 0)$.

```
           procedure binary(m, c)
           comment process all binary strings of length m
      1.     if m = 0 then process(C) else
      2.       C[m] := 0; binary(m − 1, c)
      3.       if c < k then C[m] := 1; binary(m − 1, c + 1)
```

Note that the pruning is done in line 3: If enough ones have been put into C already, then the recursion tree is pruned to prevent more ones from being put in.

507. ☞ ☺ Show that the algorithm is correct, that is, that a call to binary$(n,0)$ processes all binary strings of length n with k or fewer bits.

508. ☞ ☺ How many assignments to array C are made (that is, how often are lines 2 and 3 executed)? Hence, deduce the running time of the procedure. Is it asymptotically optimal?

The following is a backtracking algorithm for generating permutations. It fills an array $A[1..n]$ with n-ary strings, and prunes away nonpermutations by using an additional array $U[1..n]$. U is a Boolean array, with $U[i]$ set to **true** if i has not yet been used in the permutation. Initially, all entries in U are assumed to be **true**. The algorithm is used by calling permute(n).

$$
\begin{aligned}
&\textbf{procedure } \text{permute}(m) \\
&\textbf{comment } \text{process all permutations of length } m \\
1.\quad &\textbf{if } m = 0 \textbf{ then } \text{process}(A) \textbf{ else} \\
2.\quad &\quad \textbf{for } j := 1 \textbf{ to } n \textbf{ do} \\
3.\quad &\qquad \textbf{if } U[j] \textbf{ then} \\
4.\quad &\qquad\quad U[j] := \texttt{false} \\
5.\quad &\qquad\quad A[m] := j;\ \text{permute}(m-1) \\
6.\quad &\qquad\quad U[j] := \texttt{true}
\end{aligned}
$$

509. ☞ Show that the algorithm is correct, that is, that a call to permute(n) processes all permutations of length n.

510. ☞ ☀ How many assignments to array A are made (that is, how often are lines 3 and 4 executed)? Hence, deduce the running time of the procedure. Is it asymptotically optimal?

10.6 APPLICATIONS

The problems in this section are to be solved by reduction to one of the standard exhaustive search algorithms from Sections 10.1–10.4. Some of them require backtracking, and some do not.

511. ☞ ☞ A *clique* is an induced complete subgraph. The *clique problem* is the following: Given a graph G and a natural number r, does G contain a clique on r vertices? Devise an algorithm for the clique problem that runs in time $O\left(r^2 \binom{n}{r}\right)$. Briefly describe how to improve the running time by a factor of $\Omega(r)$.

512. ☜☜ ☺☞ Define the *Ramsey number* $R(i, j)$ to be the smallest number n such that every graph on n vertices has either a clique of size i or an independent set of size j. Ramsey's Theorem states that $R(i, j)$ exists for all $i, j \in \mathbb{N}$. Devise an algorithm that, given i, j, finds $R(i, j)$. Analyze your algorithm.

513. ☜☜ ☺☞ An *open knight's tour* is a sequence of $n^2 - 1$ knight's moves starting from some square of an $n \times n$ chessboard, such that every square of the board is visited exactly once. Design an algorithm for finding open knight's tours that runs in time $O(n^2 8^{n^2})$. A *closed knight's tour*, as we have seen already, is a cyclic version of an open knight's tour (that is, the start point is reachable from the finish point a single knight's move). Design an algorithm for for finding closed knight's tours that runs in time $O(8^{n^2})$.

514. ☜☜ Suppose you have n students in a class and wish to assign them into teams of two (you may assume that n is even). You are given an integer array $P[1..n, 1..n]$ in which $P[i, j]$ contains the preference of student i for working with student j. The *weight* of a pairing of student i with student j is defined to be $P[i, j] \cdot P[j, i]$. The *pairing problem* is the problem of pairing each student with another student in such a way that the sum of the weights of the pairings is maximized. Design an algorithm for the pairing problem that runs in time proportional to the number of pairings. Analyze your algorithm.

515. ☜☜ The 15-puzzle, invented by Sam Loyd, has been a source of entertainment for over a century. The puzzle consists of 15 square tiles numbered 1 through 15, arranged in row-major order in a square grid with a one-tile gap. The aim is to randomize the puzzle and then attempt to return it to the initial configuration by repeatedly sliding an adjacent tile into the gap (see, for example, Figure 10.1). The general form of this puzzle, based on an $n \times n$ grid, is called the $(n^2 - 1)$-*puzzle*. Design an algorithm that, given some configuration of the $(n^2 - 1)$-puzzle, finds a sequence of moves that return the puzzle to the initial configuration, if such a sequence of moves exists. Your algorithm should run in time $O(n^2 + 4^k)$, where k is the number of moves required for solution of the puzzle.

516. ☜☜ The following puzzle is called *Hi-Q*. You are given a board in which 33 holes have been drilled in the pattern shown in Figure 10.2. A peg (indicated by a square) is placed in every hole except the center one (indicated by a circle). Pegs are moved as follows. A peg may jump over its neighbor in the horizontal or vertical direction if its destination is unoccupied. The peg that is jumped over is removed from the board. The aim is to produce a sequence of jumps that removes all pegs from the board except for one. The generalized HI-Q puzzle has $n(n + 4m)$ holes arranged in a symmetrical cross-shape as shown in Figure 10.3, for any m and any odd n. Design an algorithm that

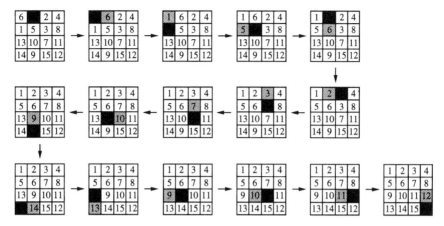

Figure 10.1. Solving the 15-puzzle.

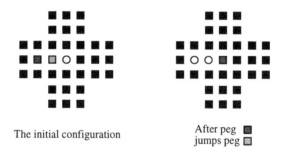

The initial configuration

After peg ▓ jumps peg ▓

Figure 10.2. The initial configuration of the Hi-Q puzzle (left), and the same configuration after a single move (right). Pegs are indicated by a square, and empty holes are indicated by a circle.

solves the Hi-Q puzzle. Let $p = n(n + 4m)$. Your algorithm should run in time $O((4p)^{p-2})$.

517. ⚓⚓ ☀ ☺⌐ The *n-queens problem* (also known as the *peaceful queens problem*) is the problem of determining the number of ways that n queens can be placed on an $n \times n$ chessboard so that no queen threatens any other (for example, Figure 10.4 shows one way of placing eight peaceful queens on an 8×8 chessboard). Devise an exhaustive search algorithm that solves the n-queens problem.

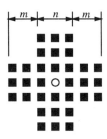

Figure 10.3. The generalized Hi-Q puzzle.

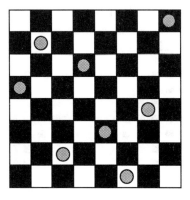

Figure 10.4. One way of placing eight peaceful queens on an 8×8 chessboard.

518. The I-C Ice Cream Company plans to place ice cream carts at strategic intersections in Dallas so that for every street intersection, either there is an ice cream cart there, or an ice cream cart can be reached by walking along only one street to the next intersection. You are given a map of Dallas in the form of a graph with nodes numbered $1, 2, \ldots, n$ representing the intersections, and undirected edges representing streets. For each ice cream cart at intersection i, the city will levy \$$c_i$ in taxes. The I-C Ice Cream Company has k ice cream carts, and can make a profit if it pays at most \$$d$ in taxes. Write a backtracking algorithm that outputs all of the possible locations for the k carts that require less than \$$d$ in taxes. Analyze your algorithm.

519. 🎓🎓 Design a backtracking algorithm that inputs a natural number C, and outputs all of the ways that a group of ascending positive numbers can be summed to give C. For example, if $C = 6$, the output should be

```
1+2+3
1+5
2+4
6
```

and if $C = 10$, the output should be

```
1+2+3+4
1+2+7
1+3+6
1+4+5
1+9
2+3+5
2+8
3+7
4+6
10
```

520. 🎓🎓 💡 📝 Devise an algorithm that, given a directed graph G, prints all Hamiltonian cycles in G. If G has n vertices, your algorithm must run in time $O(n!)$. Analyze the running time of your algorithm.

521. 🎓🎓 📝 Devise an algorithm that, given a directed graph G, prints all Hamiltonian cycles in G. If G has n vertices, your algorithm must run in time $O((n-1)!)$. Analyze the running time of your algorithm.

522. 🎓🎓 The *out-degree* of a vertex v in a graph is the number of edges directed out of v. The out-degree of a graph is the largest out-degree of its vertices. Devise a backtracking algorithm that, given a directed graph G of out-degree d, determines whether G has a Hamiltonian cycle in time $O(d^n)$. Be sure to analyze the running time of your algorithm.

523. 🎓🎓 If you were given a graph and asked to find all Hamiltonian cycles in it, which algorithm would you use, the algorithm from Problem 520 or the algorithm from Problem 522? Explain your answer.

A *dominating set* of size k in a graph $G = (V, E)$ is a set $U \subseteq V$ of k vertices such that for all $v \in V$, either $v \in U$, or there exists an edge $(u, v) \in E$ such that $u \in U$. For example, the shaded vertices in the graph of Figure 10.5 form a dominating set.

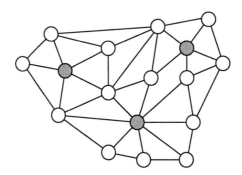

Figure 10.5. A dominating set (shaded vertices).

524. ☞ Let $D(n, k)$ be the number of candidates for a dominating set in an exhaustive search algorithm. Write a formula for $D(n, k)$ in terms of n and k.

525. ☞☞ 💡 Devise an algorithm that, given G and k, finds a dominating set of size k, if one exists. Your algorithm should run in time $O(n^2 D(n, k))$. Analyze the running time of your algorithm.

526. ☞☞ 💡 Describe how to improve the running time of your algorithm to $O(nD(n, k))$. Justify briefly the running time of your modified algorithm.

A *weighing matrix* is an $n \times n$ matrix with entries from $\{-1, 0, 1\}$ such that the scalar product of any two rows is zero. That is, a matrix

$$M = \begin{bmatrix} m_{1,1} & m_{1,2} & \cdots & m_{1,n} \\ m_{2,1} & m_{2,2} & \cdots & m_{2,n} \\ & & \ddots & \\ m_{n,1} & m_{n,2} & \cdots & m_{n,n} \end{bmatrix},$$

where for all $1 \leq j \leq n$ and all $1 \leq i < j$,

$$\sum_{k=1}^{n} m_{i,k} m_{j,k} = 0.$$

527. ☞☞ 💡 Design an algorithm that finds all $n \times n$ weighing matrices in time $O(n^3 3^{n^2})$. Analyze your algorithm.

528. ☞☞ 💡 Describe how to reduce the running time of your algorithm to $O(n3^{n^2})$.

Preference Matrices:

$$P \quad \begin{array}{cccc} 1 & 2 & 3 & 4 \end{array}$$

	1	2	3	4
1	2	3	1	1
2	1	1	4	3
3	1	2	3	4
4	2	3	2	1

$$N \quad \begin{array}{cccc} 1 & 2 & 3 & 4 \end{array}$$

	1	2	3	4
1	4	1	3	2
2	4	2	3	1
3	1	1	1	4
4	3	2	3	3

Candidate Matching:

Pilot: 1 2 3 4

Navigator: 1 2 3 4

Weight: P[1,2]N[2,1]+P[2,4]N[4,2]+P[3,1]N[1,3]+P[4,3]N[3,4]
         = 3·4+3·2+1·3+2·4 = 12+6+3+8 = 29

Figure 10.6. The preference matrices P and N (top), a candidate matching (center), and the sum of the weights of the pairs in this matching (bottom).

Suppose you are given n pilots and n navigators. You have an integer array $P[1..n, 1..n]$ in which $P[i,j]$ is the preference of pilot i for navigator j, and an integer array $N[1..n, 1..n]$ in which $N[i,j]$ is the preference of navigator i for pilot j. The *weight* of a pairing of pilot i with navigator j is defined to be $P[i,j] \cdot N[j,i]$. The *flight-assignment problem* is the problem of pairing each pilot with a navigator in such a way that the sum of the weights of the pairings is maximized. Figure 10.6 shows an example of the preference arrays, a candidate matching, and the sum of the weights of the pairs in this matching:

529. Design an algorithm for the flight-assignment problem that runs in time $O((n+1)!)$. Analyze your algorithm.

530. Describe how to improve the running time of your algorithm from Problem 529 to $O(n!)$.

The *postage stamp problem* is defined as follows. The Fussytown Post Office has n different denominations of stamps, each a positive integer. Fussytown regulations allow at most m stamps to be placed on any letter.

531. ☜☞ Design an algorithm that, given n different postage stamp values in an array $P[1..n]$ and the value of m, computes the length of the consecutive series of postage values that can legally be realized under these rules starting with the value 1. For example, if $n = 4$, $m = 5$, and the stamps have face value $1, 4, 12$, and 21, then all postage values from 1 to 71 can be realized. Your algorithm should run in time $O(n^m)$.

Figure 10.7. The 4-ominos.

532. ☞☞ Design an algorithm that, given n and m, computes the m postage stamp values that can realize the longest consecutive run of postage values starting at 1. Analyze your algorithm.

A *polyomino*, or more precisely, an *n-omino* is a plane figure made up of n unit-size squares lined up on a grid. For example, Figure 10.7 shows all of the 4-ominos.

533. ☞☞ Design an algorithm that runs in time $O(3^n)$ to generate all n-ominos, including all rotations and reflections.

534. ☞☞ Modify your algorithm to remove all rotations and reflections.

10.7 HINTS

487. Be very careful how you choose your recurrence relation. The obvious choice of recurrence is quite difficult to solve. The right choice can make it easy.

489. Suppose that $A[i] = i$ for $1 \le i \le n$, and pretend that procedure process(A) prints the contents of A. Trace the algorithm by hand to see what it generates when $n = 1, 2, 3, 4$. This should give you some intuition as to how it works, what your induction hypothesis should be, and how the basic structure of your proof should look.

491. See the hint for Problem 489. Your induction hypothesis should look something like the following:
When n is even, a call to evenpermute(n)

  - processes all permutations of the values in $A[1..n]$, and
  - finishes with the entries in A permuted in some order in which, if repeated $n-1$ times, cycles $A[1]$ through all possible values from 1 to n. Determining and describing this permutation is the difficult part.

When n is odd, a call to oddpermute(n)

  - processes all permutations of the values in $A[1..n]$, and
  - finishes with the first and last entries in A swapped.

502. You may need to use the identity from Problem 23.

510. The answer is at most $1.718(n + 1)!$. You will need to use the fact that $\sum_{i=1}^{n} i! = e - 1 \approx 1.718$ (where e is the base of the natural logarithm).

518. Think about dominating sets.

517. It is possible to solve this problem in time $O(n!)$.

520. The running time gives away the technique to be used. Reduce the problem to that of generating permutations.

525. Reduce the problem to that of generating combinations, and take advantage of Section 10.3.

526. Use a minimal-change algorithm.

527. Use the algorithm from Problem 480.

528. See Problem 483.

10.8   SOLUTIONS

487. Let $T(n)$ be the running time of permute(n). Line 6 can be done in time $O(n)$. Therefore, $T(1) = c$, and for $n > 2$, $T(n) = nT(n - 1) + d(n - 1)$, for some $c, d \in \mathbb{N}$. We claim that for all $n \geq 1$, $T(n) = (c + d)n! - d$. The proof is by induction on n. The claim is certainly true for $n = 1$, since $T(1) = c$ and $(c + d)1! - d = c$. Now suppose the hypothesis is true for n. Then,

$$
\begin{aligned}
T(n + 1) &= (n + 1)T(n) + dn \\
&= (n + 1)((c + d)n! - d) + dn \\
&= (c + d)(n + 1)! - d.
\end{aligned}
$$

Hence, the running time is $O(n!)$, which is linear in the number of permutations.

520. The following algorithm prints all of the Hamiltonian cycles of a graph G.

for each permutation $P[0..n-1]$ **do**
  process(P)

procedure process(P)
  if hamiltonian(P) **then** print(P)

function hamiltonian(P):boolean
  ok:=true
  for $i := 0$ **to** $n-1$ **do**
    ok:=ok $\land$ $(P[i], P[(i+1) \bmod n]) \in E$
  return(ok)

We use an optimal permutation generation algorithm such as one of the algorithms from Section 10.2. Since function hamiltonian(P) takes time $O(n)$, the search takes time $O(n \cdot n!)$. The running time can be reduced to $O(n!)$ by observing that all of the permutations can begin with vertex 1.

521. The solution is similar to the solution of Problem 520, but we use a minimal-change algorithm such as Heap's algorithm (see Section 10.2) to generate permutations.

We keep a Boolean array $D[0..n-1]$, where $D[i]$ is true iff $(P[i], P[(i+1) \bmod n]) \in E$, for $0 \le i < n$, and a count of missing edges, called "missing." We initialize the array and count when processing the first permutation. A minimal change to P requires a minimal change to the array and the count. Procedure process is exactly as in the solution to Problem 520.

  missing:=0
  P:= first permutation
  process(P)
  for each permutation P in minimal-change order **do**
    Suppose $P[x]$ and $P[y]$ were just swapped
    iprocess(P, x, y)

procedure edge(i, j)
  $D[i] := (i,j) \in E$
  if $(i,j) \notin E$ **then** missing:=missing+1

procedure iprocess(P, x, y)
  if ihamiltonian(P, x, y) **then** print(P)

function ihamiltonian(P, x, y):boolean
  iedge($P[(x-1) \bmod n], P[x]$);
  iedge($P[x], P[(x+1) \bmod n]$);
  iedge($P[(y-1) \bmod n], P[y]$);
  iedge($P[y], P[(y+1) \bmod n]$);
  return(missing $= 0$)

procedure iedge(i, j)
if $D[i] \wedge ((i, j) \notin E)$ **then**
  $D[i]$:=false; missing:=missing $+ 1$
else if (not $D[i]) \wedge ((i, j) \in E)$ **then**
  $D[i]$:=true; missing:=missing $- 1$

The time needed to process the first permutation is $O(n)$. The other $n! - 1$ permutations require $O(1)$ time each to process. The overhead for generating the permutations is $O(n!)$ with a minimal-change algorithm such as Heap's algorithm. Therefore, the total running time is $O(n + (n! - 1) + n!) = O(n!)$. As before, this running time can be reduced by a factor of $\Omega(n)$ by observing that all of the permutations can begin with vertex 1.

10.9 COMMENTS

478. The algorithm generates the binary reflected Gray code (see also Problems 96 and 97).

497. The algorithm is adapted from Lam and Soicher [51]. You will find a correctness proof there, but there is an easier and clearer explanation. Another interesting algorithm with a stronger minimal-change property is given by Eades and McKay [23].

507. See also Problem 474.

508. See also Problem 475.

512. For more information on Ramsey numbers, consult Graham and Spencer [32], and Graham, Rothschild, and Spencer [31].

513. See also Problems 48 and 369 (and associated comments), which deal with closed knight's tours. Backtracking for $n \times n$ closed knight's tours is only practical for $n = 6$ (there are no tours for smaller n), in which case there are 9,862 closed knight's tours. It is not known exactly how many 8×8 tours exist. Rouse Ball and Coxeter [8] describe an interesting random walk algorithm that they attribute to Euler. A heuristic attributed to Warnsdorff in 1823 by Conrad, Hindrichs, Morsy, and Wegener [15, 16] appears to help both the exhaustive search and random walk algorithms find solutions faster: When there is a choice of squares to move to, move to the one with the least number of unused legal moves out of it. Takefuji and Lee [79] (reprinted in Takefuji [78, Chapter 7]) describe a neural network for finding closed knight's tours, but empirical evidence indicates that their algorithm is impractical (Parberry [62]).

517. Although an algorithm that runs in time $O(n!)$ is considered very slow, it

n	count	time
6	4	< 0.001 seconds
7	40	< 0.001 seconds
8	92	< 0.001 seconds
9	352	0.034 seconds
10	724	0.133 seconds
11	2,680	0.6 seconds
12	14,200	3.3 seconds
13	73,712	18.0 seconds
14	365,596	1.8 minutes
15	2,279,184	11.6 minutes
16	14,772,512	1.3 hours
17	95,815,104	9.1 hours
18	666,090,624	2.8 days

Table 10.1. The number of solutions to the n-queens problem for $6 \leq n \leq 18$ and the running time required to exhaustively search for them using a naive exhaustive search algorithm. The algorithm was implemented in Berkeley Unix Pascal on a Sun Sparc 2.

is still usable in practice for very small n. Table 10.1 shows the number of solutions to the n-queens problem and the running time required to find them using Berkeley Unix Pascal on Sun Sparc 2. It is known that there is at least one solution to the n-queens problem for all $n \geq 4$ (see, for example, Bernhardsson [11]). Heuristics for finding large numbers of solutions (but not necessarily all of them) include Takefuji [78], and Susic and Gu [77].

518. This problem was described to me by Mike Fellows.

Chapter 11

Data Structures

Algorithms and data structures are obviously very closely related. Firstly, you must understand algorithms in order to design data structures, since an important issue in choosing a particular data structure is the availability of efficient algorithms for creating, updating, and accessing it. Secondly, you must understand data structures in order to design algorithms, since the proper organization of data is often the key to developing efficient algorithms. Some schools separate algorithms and data structures into separate classes, but I prefer to teach them together. In case your algorithms class requires it, here are some problems on advanced data structures, principally heaps, binary search trees, AVL trees, 2–3 trees, and the union-find data structure.

11.1 HEAPS

A *heap* is a binary tree with the data stored in the nodes. It has two important properties: *balance* and *structure*. *Balance* means that it is as much like a complete binary tree as possible. Missing leaves, if any, are on the last level at the far right (see, for example, Figure 11.1). *Structure* means that the value in each parent is no greater than the values in its children (see, for example, Figure 11.2).

535. 🎓 🐿 Prove that the value in each node is no greater than the values in its descendants (that is, its children, its children's children, etc.)

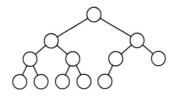

Figure 11.1. A balanced binary tree.

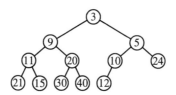

Figure 11.2. A heap.

536. ☞ Prove by induction that a heap with n vertices has exactly $\lceil n/2 \rceil$ leaves.

537. ☞ 🔦 ☺☞ Suppose a heap is stored in an array H in the standard fashion. That is, store the root in $H[1]$, and for every node stored in $H[k]$, store its children in $H[2k]$ and $H[2k+1]$. Prove that an n-node heap occupies the first n contiguous entries of H.

538. ☞ Suppose a heap is stored in an array H in the standard fashion (see Problem 537). Prove that a list of the array elements $H[1], H[2], \ldots, H[n]$ form a breadth-first traversal of the heap.

539. ☞ Devise a divide-and-conquer algorithm (see Chapter 7) for building a heap stored in an array $H[1..n]$ in $O(n)$ time.

540. ☞ Give the array representation heap shown in Figure 11.2, and redraw the heap and its array representation after each of the following operations have been applied in sequence:

(a) `deletemin`, followed by

(b) `insert` the value 0.

541. ☞ Construct a heap containing the items 10, 2, 9, 16, 8, 6, 1, 3, 12. You are to draw the heap (as a binary tree) at each of the major steps in the construction.

(a) Inserting the items in the order given into an empty heap.

(b) Building the heap from the bottom up, as in *heapsort*.

542. ☞ Write a procedure that, given parameters A, n, and i, where A is the array representation of an n-element heap, and $1 \le i \le n$, deletes the element $A[i]$ from the heap in $O(\log n)$ time.

543. ☞ ☞ *Halving* is the process of taking a set S of integers and separating it into two half-sized sets S_1, S_2, where all of the values in S_1 are smaller than all of the values in S_2. Show that halving is equivalent to finding the median, that is:

(a) If the median can be found using $T(n)$ comparisons, then a set of size n can be halved with $T(n) + n - 1$ comparisons.

(b) If a set of size n can be halved using $T(n)$ comparisons, then the median can be found using $T(n) + \lceil n/2 \rceil - 1$ comparisons.

544. ☜☜ ▦ Devise a data structure that supports the following operations on an n-element set: `insert` in time $O(\log n)$, and `deletemin` and `deletemax` in $O(1)$ time.

The standard heapsort algorithm uses binary heaps, that is, heaps in which each node has at most two children. In a k-ary heap, each node has at most k children. Heapsort works not only with binary heaps, but with k-ary heaps for any $k = 1, 2, 3, \ldots$.

545. ☜ ▱ Define k-ary heaps and describe a space-efficient implementation in an array. In particular, describe in detail how to get from any heap element to its parent and its k children.

546. ☜ Write pseudocode for k-ary heapsort.

547. ☜ What familiar sorting algorithm is k-ary heapsort for $k = 1$?

548. ☜☜ For $k > 1$, analyze the number of binary comparisons used by k-ary heapsort in terms of n and k, determining the coefficient (depending on k) of the most significant n-term. Which k minimizes this factor? Why is $k = 2$ probably best anyway?

A *parallel priority queue* is a priority queue in which the `insert` operation inserts p values, and the `deletemin` operation deletes the p smallest values in the priority queue and returns them in no particular order. A *parallel heap* is a data structure with the same tree structure as a heap, but with p values per node. It also has the property that all of the values in a node are smaller than the values in its children, and all of the values in one sibling are smaller than the values in the other (it doesn't matter which is the "smaller" sibling). For example, Figure 11.3 shows a parallel heap with $p = 4$.

Sequential algorithms for parallel heaps are fairly straightforward: An `insert` operation is processed by first placing the p new items in the next unused node d, which we will call *dirty*. Combine the values in d and its parent r, and place the smallest p values into r, and the largest p values into d. Combine the values in d and its sibling (if it has one), and place the largest p values into the sibling that had the largest value between them, and the smallest p values into the other sibling. Node r then becomes the dirty node, which is processed in a similar fashion. For example, Figure 11.4 shows an insertion into a 4-node parallel heap with $p = 4$.

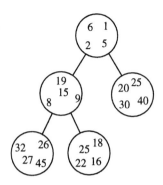

Figure 11.3. A parallel heap with $p = 4$.

A `deletemin` operation is processed by removing the values from the root and replacing them with the values from the last used node. Call the root *dirty*. Let d be the dirty node. Combine the values in d with those of its smallest child s, and place the smallest p values into d and the largest p values into s. Combine the values in d and its sibling (if it has one), and place the largest p values into the sibling that had the largest value between them, and the smallest p values into the other sibling. Node s then becomes the dirty node, which is processed in a similar fashion.

549. ☞ ☞ Show that the `insert` algorithm is correct, that is, it results in a parallel heap.

550. ☞ ☞ Show that the `deletemin` algorithm, that is, it results in a parallel heap.

551. ☞ ☞ 💡 Analyze the running time of the `insert` and `deletemin` algorithms.

11.2 AVL TREES

A *binary search tree* is a binary tree with the data stored in the nodes. The following two properties hold:

- The value in each node is larger than the values in the nodes of its left subtree.
- The value in each node is smaller than the values in the nodes of its right subtree.

552. ☞ Prove that if the nodes of a binary search tree are printed in in-order, they come out sorted.

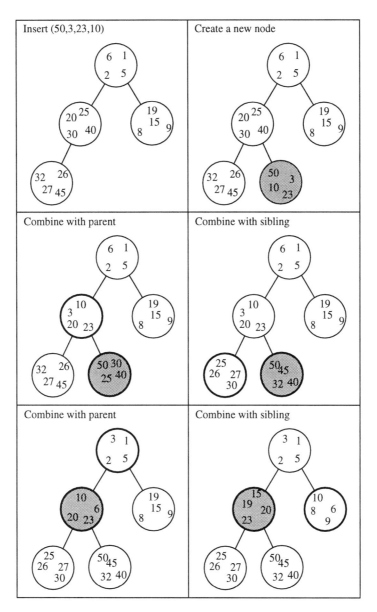

Figure 11.4. An insertion into a 4-node parallel heap with $p = 4$. Heavily outlined nodes have been combined. The dirty node is shaded.

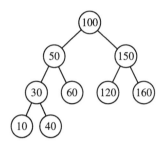

Figure 11.5. An AVL tree.

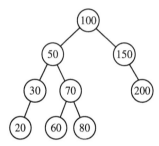

Figure 11.6. A second AVL tree.

An *AVL tree* is a binary search tree with one extra structure condition: For every node, the magnitude of the difference in height between its left and right subtrees is at most one. (the *height* of an AVL tree is the number of edges in the longest path from the root to a leaf). This difference in height is maintained during insertions and deletions using operations called *single rotations* and *double rotations*. Operations insert, delete, member, and findmin can be performed in time $O(\log n)$.

553. ☞ Insert 5 into the AVL tree shown in Figure 11.5.

554. ☞ Insert 55 into the AVL tree shown in Figure 11.6.

555. ☞ Delete 30 from the AVL tree shown in Figure 11.7.

556. ☞ Find an AVL tree for which the deletion of a node requires two single rotations. Draw the tree, indicate the node to be deleted, and explain why two rotations are necessary and sufficient.

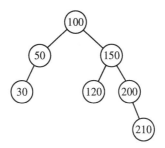

Figure 11.7. A third AVL tree.

557. ☞ Find an AVL tree for which the deletion of a node requires two double
     rotations. Draw the tree, indicate the node to be deleted, and explain why
     two rotations are necessary and sufficient.

558. ☞ ☞ Show that for all $n \in \mathbb{N}$, there exists an AVL tree for which the
     deletion of a node requires n (single or double) rotations. Show how such
     a tree is constructed, indicate the node to be deleted, and explain why n
     rotations are necessary and sufficient.

559. ☞ ☞ 💡 ☞ Prove that the height of an AVL tree with n nodes is at most
     $1.4404 \log n$.

11.3 2–3 TREES

A *2–3 tree* in a tree in which every internal vertex has 2 or 3 children, and every
path from the root to a leaf has the same length. The data are stored in the leaves in
sorted order from left to right. The internal nodes carry information to allow searching, for example, the largest values in the left and center subtrees. Insertions and
deletions are performed using a divide-and-conquer algorithm. Operations `insert`,
`delete`, `member` and `findmin` can be performed in time $O(\log n)$.

560. ☞ Insert the following elements in sequence into an initially empty 2–3
     tree: $5, 2, 7, 0, 3, 4, 6, 1, 8, 9$. Show the 2–3 tree after every insertion. Be sure
     to include all of the information that is kept in the internal nodes. Delete the
     element 3 from the resulting 2–3 tree.

561. ☞ Give a sequence of insertions and deletions that constructs the 2–3 trees
     shown in Figure 11.8 (starting from the empty 2–3 tree each time). Draw the
     2–3 tree after every insertion and deletion operation.

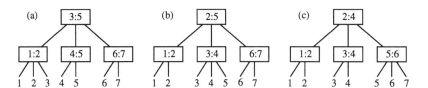

Figure 11.8. Three 2–3 trees.

11.4   THE UNION-FIND PROBLEM

Given a set $\{1, 2, \ldots, n\}$ initially partitioned into n disjoint subsets, one member per subset, we want to perform the following operations:

- find(x): return the name of the subset that x is in, and
- union(x, y): combine the two subsets that x and y are in.

There is a standard data structure using a tree. Use a tree:

- implemented with pointers and records;
- set elements are stored in the nodes;
- each child has a pointer to its parent;
- there is an array $P[1..n]$ with $P[i]$ pointing to the node containing i.

There is an algorithm for union and find operations that works in worst-case time $O(\log n)$ and amortized time $O(log^*n)$.

562. ☞☞ ☀ Design an algorithm that can perform a sequence m union and find operations on a Universal set of n elements, consisting of a sequence of unions followed by a sequence of finds, in time $O(m + n)$.

Suppose we modify the union-find algorithm so that the root of the shallower tree points to the root of the deeper tree (instead of the root of the smaller tree pointing to the root of the deeper tree).

563. ☞ Does this affect the running time of the algorithm in the worst case?

564. ☞☞ Does it affect the amortized running time when path compression is used?

11.5   APPLICATIONS

This section asks you to use your knowledge of data structures to design algorithms for new problems.

565. ☞ Design a data structure for a set in which insertions, deletions, and membership queries can be processed in $O(1)$ time in the worst case. You may assume that the set elements are integers drawn from a finite set $\{1, 2, \ldots, n\}$.

566. ☞ ☞ Let $S = \{s_1, s_2, \ldots, s_\ell\}$ and $T = \{t_1, t_2, \ldots, t_m\}$ be two sets of integers such that $1 \le s_i, t_j \le n$ for all $1 \le i \le \ell$ and $1 \le j \le m$. Design an algorithm for determining whether $S = T$ in time $O(\ell + m)$.

567. ☞ ☞ ✍ Design an implementation of the following Abstract Data Type: a set with the operations:

insert(x, T)	Insert item x into the set T.
delete(k, T)	Delete the kth smallest element from T.
member(x, T)	Return true iff $x \in T$.

All operations on an n item set are to take time $O(\log n)$.

568. ☞ ☞ Design an implementation of the following Abstract Data Type: a set with the operations:

insert(x, T)	Insert item x into the set T.
delete(x, T)	Delete x from T.
member(x, T)	Return true iff $x \in T$.
next(x, T)	Return the smallest element of T greater than x
union(S, T)	Set S to the union of S and T.

The operations insert, delete, member, and next are to take time $O(\log n)$, and union is to take time $O(n)$.

569. ☞ ☞ Design an implementation of an Abstract Data Type consisting of a set with the following operations:

insert(S, x)	Insert x into the set S.
delete(S, x)	Delete x from the set S.
member(S, x)	Return true if $x \in S$, false otherwise.
position(S, x)	Return the number of elements of S less than x.
concatenate(S, T)	Set S to the union of S and T, assuming every element in S is smaller than every element of T.

All operations involving n-element sets are to take time $O(\log n)$.

570. ☞ ☞ The *bin packing problem* is the following. You are given n metal objects, each weighing between zero and one kilogram. You also have a collection of large, but fragile bins. Your aim is to find the smallest number of bins that will hold the n objects, with no bin holding more than one kilogram.

The *first-fit heuristic* for the bin packing problem is the following. Take each of the objects in the order in which they are given. For each object, scan the bins in increasing order of remaining capacity, and place it into the first bin in which it fits. Design an algorithm that implements the first-fit heuristic (taking as input the n weights $w_1, w_2, \ldots, w_n$ and outputting the number of bins needed when using first-fit) in $O(n \log n)$ time.

571. ☞☞ Suppose $(A, \cdot)$ is a semigroup, where $A = \{a_1, \ldots, a_n\}$. (That is, A is closed under "·", and "·" is associative.) Devise a data structure that allows you to compute $a_i \cdot a_{i+1} \cdots a_j$ for any $i \leq j$ in only $O(\log n)$ semigroup operations.

572. ☞☞ Reduce the running time in Problem 571 to $O(1)$ when $(A, \cdot)$ is a group, and group inversion is allowed for free.

573. ☞☞☞ The Dallas Tollway uses a computerized toll collection system. The highway is modeled as as an ordered list of toll booths $t_1, t_2, \ldots, t_n$ in which toll booth t_i collects a toll of $\$a_i$, for $1 \leq i \leq n$. Design a data structure that can perform the following operations in $O(\log n)$ time.

insert(k, a)	Insert a new toll booth after t_k with toll $\$a$.
delete(k)	Delete toll booth t_k.
toll(i, j)	Return total toll for booths i through j, inclusive.
update(i, j, a)	Add $\$a$ to the toll for booths i through j, inclusive.

574. ☞☞ Suppose we are to support a set of ordered pairs (p, k), where k is an integer key and p is an integer priority. Devise a data structure in which the following operations can be implemented in $O(\log n)$ time:

insert(p, k)	Insert item with priority p and key k
member(k)	Return item of smallest priority among those with key $\leq k$.
delete(k)	Delete all items with key k.

You are to design a memory-efficient data structure that is constructed from a sequence of n values $x_1, x_2, \ldots, x_n$, and can quickly answer queries of the form: "Given i, j, find the smallest value in $x_i, \ldots, x_j$."

575. ☞☞ Design a data structure that uses $O(n \log n)$ space and answers queries in $O(\log n)$ time.

576. ☞☞ Design a data structure that uses $O(n)$ space and answers queries in $O(\log n)$ time.

577. 🎓 🎓 Use your solution to Problem 576 to design a data structure to quickly answer least-common-ancestor queries in a tree. That is, your data structure will be constructed from a description of a tree, and using this data structure you must answer queries of the form: "What is the least-common-ancestor of tree vertices v and w?"

11.6 HINTS

535. Prove it by induction on level.

537. Prove it by induction on n.

544. Use two heaps A and B, each containing $\lceil n/2 \rceil$ elements (if n is odd, store one item separately). Make A a min-heap, B a max-heap, and ensure that for each $1 \le i \le \lceil n/2 \rceil$, $A[i] \le B[i]$. Then, the root of A will be the smallest value and the root of B will be the largest value.

551. See Problem 543.

559. Let $N(h)$ be the minimum number of nodes in an AVL tree of height h. Devise a recurrence relation for a lower bound for $N(h)$ (start with $N(0) = 1$, $N(1) = 2$). Show that this recurrence has solution

$$N(h) > \left(\frac{1 + \sqrt{5}}{2} \right)^h.$$

562. It's the standard union-find algorithm with path compression. The difficult part is the amortized analysis.

570 You will need a data structure that allows you to find the "first bin in which it fits" in time $O(\log n)$.

11.7 SOLUTIONS

545. A k-ary heap is a k-ary tree with the data stored in the nodes. It has two important properties: *balance* and *structure*. *Balance* means that it is as much like a complete k-ary tree as possible. Missing leaves, if any, are on the last level at the far right. *Structure* means that the value in each parent is no greater than the values in its children. A k-ary heap on n vertices can be efficiently implemented in storage using contiguous locations of a linear array $A[1..n]$, such that the root of the heap is stored in $A[1]$, the vertices are stored in level order, and for any level, the vertices in it are stored in left-to-right

order. It can be shown that the parent of $A[m]$ is $A[\lfloor (m+k-2)/k \rfloor]$ and its children are $A[km-k+2], \ldots, A[\min(km+1, n)]$.

559. Let $N(h)$ be the minimum number of nodes in an AVL tree of height h. Clearly, $N(0) = 1$ and $N(1) = 2$, and for $h \geq 2$, $N(h) > N(h-1) + N(h-2)$. We claim that $N(h) \geq c^h$ for some choice of c. The proof is by induction on h. The claim is true for $h \leq 2$ provided $c < 2$. For $h > 2$, by the induction hypothesis,
$$N(h) > N(h-1) + N(h-2) \geq c^{h-1} + c^{h-2}.$$

So we need (assuming $c > 0$) $c^2 - c - 1 \leq 0$. The largest value of c for which this is true is $(1 + \sqrt{5})/2$. Therefore, by induction,
$$N(h) > \left(\frac{1 + \sqrt{5}}{2}\right)^h.$$

What is the height of an AVL tree with n nodes? We know that
$$n \geq N(h) > \left(\frac{1 + \sqrt{5}}{2}\right)^h.$$

Therefore,
$$h < \frac{\log n}{\log((1 + \sqrt{5})/2)} \approx 1.4404 \log n.$$

567. We use a 2–3 tree augmented with extra fields in each internal node recording how many leaves are descendants of the left, middle, and right children. The insertion is done as normal, with extra code to increment the leaf-count of the nodes on the path from the root to the new leaf, and to take care of the new fields during node splitting. The deletion code is modified in a similar way, with the extra modification that the location of the leaf to be deleted is done using the new leaf-count fields in the obvious way (recall that in a 2–3 tree, the leaves are in ascending order from left to right). The member operations are done as normal.

11.8 COMMENTS

537. You'll see this result in all competent data structures textbooks, but you'll seldom see a proof of it.

570. This problem is $\mathcal{NP}$-complete (see Chapter 12 if you don't know what this means), and so it is unlikely that there is a polynomial-time algorithm for finding an exact solution.

Chapter 12

$\mathcal{NP}$-**completeness**

Define $\mathcal{P}$ to be the set of decision problems (that is, problems that have a yes/no answer) that can be solved in polynomial time. If x is a bit string, let $|x|$ denote the number of bits in x. Define $\mathcal{NP}$ to be the set of decision problems of the following form, where $R \in \mathcal{P}$, $c \in \mathbf{N}$: "Given x, does there exist y with $|y| \leq |x|^c$ such that $(x, y) \in R$." That is, $\mathcal{NP}$ is the set of existential questions that can be *verified* in polynomial time. Clearly, $\mathcal{P} \subseteq \mathcal{NP}$. It is not known whether $\mathcal{P} = \mathcal{NP}$, although the consensus of opinion is that probably $\mathcal{P} \neq \mathcal{NP}$. But it is known that there are problems in $\mathcal{NP}$ with the property that if they are members of $\mathcal{P}$, then $\mathcal{P} = \mathcal{NP}$. That is, if anything in $\mathcal{NP}$ is outside of $\mathcal{P}$, then they are, too. They are called $\mathcal{NP}$-*complete* problems.

A problem A is *reducible* to B if an algorithm for B can be used to solve A. More specifically, if there is an algorithm that maps every instance x of A into an instance $f(x)$ of B such that $x \in A$ iff $f(x) \in B$. A problem A is *polynomial time reducible* to B, written $A \leq_p^m B$, if there is a polynomial time algorithm that maps every instance x of A into an instance $f(x)$ of B such that $x \in A$ iff $f(x) \in B$. Note that the size of $f(x)$ can be no greater than a polynomial of the size of x.

Listing problems on $\mathcal{NP}$-completeness is a little bit redundant. The truly dedicated student can practice by picking two random $\mathcal{NP}$-complete problems from the long list in the back of Garey and Johnson [28] and attempting to prove that one is reducible to the other. But here are a few problems that I find useful.

12.1   GENERAL

This section contains a few general questions about $\mathcal{NP}$-completeness. Many of them use variants of the *satisfiability problem*. The standard terminology is used here: A *literal* is a complemented or uncomplemented variable, a *clause* is a disjunction of literals, and a *Boolean formula* is a conjunction of clauses. Then SAT is defined as follows:

> SAT
>
> INSTANCE: A Boolean formula F.

QUESTION: Is there a truth assignment to the variables of F that makes F true?

578. ☜ ☺☞ Prove that "$\leq_p^m$" is transitive, that is, if $A \leq_p^m B$ and $B \leq_p^m C$, then $A \leq_p^m C$.

579. ☜☜ 2SAT is the satisfiability problem with at most two literals per clause. Show that 2SAT $\in \mathcal{P}$.

580. ☜ A *monom* is a conjunction of literals. A Boolean formula in *disjunctive normal form* is a disjunction of monoms. Consider the following problem:

DNF SAT
INSTANCE: A Boolean formula F in disjunctive normal form.
QUESTION: Is there a truth assignment to the variables of F that makes F true?

Prove that DNF SAT $\in \mathcal{P}$.

581. ☜☜ Show that the following problem can be solved in polynomial time:

STRONG 3SAT
INSTANCE: A Boolean formula F in conjunctive normal form with at most three literals per clause.
QUESTION: Is there a truth assignment to the variables of F that makes at least two literals in each clause of F true?

582. ☜☜ Show that the following problem can be solved in polynomial time:

PARITY 3SAT
INSTANCE: A Boolean formula F in conjunctive normal form with at most three literals per clause.
QUESTION: Is there a truth assignment to the variables of F that makes an odd number of literals in each clause of F true?

12.2 COOK REDUCTIONS

The definition of "reduction" used in the preamble to this chapter is the one most commonly used in algorithms classes. Technically, it is called a *polynomial time many-one reduction* or a *Karp reduction* (after Karp [43]).

There is another definition of reducibility that you will meet in the literature if you read more about $\mathcal{NP}$-completeness. A problem A is *polynomial time Turing reducible* to B, written $A \leq_p^T B$, if there is an algorithm for B that calls the algorithm for A as a subroutine, and this algorithm makes polynomially many calls to A and runs in polynomial time if the calls to A are not counted. This type of reduction is sometimes called a *Cook reduction* after Cook [17].

583. ☞ Prove that if $A \leq_p^T B$ and $B \in \mathcal{P}$, then $A \in \mathcal{P}$.

584. ☞ Prove that if $B \in \mathcal{NP}$ and for all $A \in \mathcal{NP}$, $A \leq_p^T B$, then B is $\mathcal{NP}$-complete.

585. ☞ Prove that "$\leq_p^T$" is transitive, that is, if $A \leq_p^T B$ and $B \leq_p^T C$, then $A \leq_p^T C$.

586. ☞ Prove that if $B \leq_p^T C$, $C \in \mathcal{NP}$, and B is $\mathcal{NP}$-complete, then C is $\mathcal{NP}$-complete.

Consider the following two versions of the satisfiability problem.

SAT1
INSTANCE: A Boolean formula F.
QUESTION: Is there a truth assignment to the variables of F that makes F true?

SAT2
INSTANCE: A Boolean formula F.
OUTPUT: A truth assignment to the variables of F that makes F true, if one exists.

The former is the decision problem for satisfiability, and the second requires the construction of a solution. Clearly the decision problem is Cook reducible to the solution problem. The term *self-reducibility*, coined by Mike Paterson, is used to describe problems for which the opposite is true.

587. ☞☞ Show that SAT2 $\leq_p^T$ SAT1.

Consider the following variants of the traveling salesperson problem:

TSP1
INSTANCE: A directed graph G with positive costs on the edges, and a positive integer B.
QUESTION: Is there a Hamiltonian cycle in G of cost at most B?

TSP2
INSTANCE: A directed graph G with positive costs on the edges, and a positive integer B.
OUTPUT: A Hamiltonian cycle in G of cost at most B, if one exists.

TSP3

INSTANCE: A directed graph G with positive costs on the edges, and a positive integer B.

OUTPUT: A Hamiltonian cycle in G of minimum cost, if one exists.

588.   ☜ ☜ Prove that TSP2 $\leq_p^T$ TSP1.

589.   ☜ ☜ Prove that TSP3 $\leq_p^T$ TSP2.

590.   ☜ ☜ Prove directly that TSP3 $\leq_p^T$ TSP1, without using the fact that "$\leq_p^T$" is transitive.

12.3 WHAT IS WRONG?

Scientists have been working since the early 1970s to either prove or disprove that $\mathcal{P} \neq \mathcal{NP}$. This open problem is rapidly gaining popularity as one of the leading mathematical open problems today (ranking with Fermat's last theorem and the Reimann hypothesis). There are several incorrect proofs that $\mathcal{P} = \mathcal{NP}$ announced every year. What is wrong with the following proofs that $\mathcal{P} = \mathcal{NP}$?

591.   ☜ ☺☞ It is known that the dominating set problem (see also Problem 523) remains $\mathcal{NP}$-complete even when the dominating set is required to be connected (see, for example, Garey and Johnson [28]). The interior nodes of a breadth-first search tree form a connected dominating set. For each vertex v of a graph $G = (V, E)$ with n vertices and e edges, find the breadth-first search tree rooted at v in time $O(n+e)$. Then, pick the tree with the smallest number of interior vertices. These form a minimum-size connected dominating set, found in time $O(ne + n^2)$. Hence, $\mathcal{P} = \mathcal{NP}$.

592.   ☜ It is known that 3SAT is $\mathcal{NP}$-complete. Given a Boolean formula in conjunctive normal form with at most three literals per clause, use the distributive law to construct an equivalent formula in disjunctive normal form. For example,

$$(x_1 \vee x_2 \vee \overline{x}_3) \wedge (\overline{x}_1 \vee \overline{x}_2) = (x_1 \wedge \overline{x}_2) \vee (x_2 \wedge \overline{x}_1) \vee (\overline{x}_3 \wedge \overline{x}_1) \vee (\overline{x}_3 \wedge \overline{x}_2).$$

Since DNF-SAT $\in \mathcal{P}$ (see Problem 580), a satisfying assignment for the new formula, and hence for the old formula, can be found in polynomial time. This shows that 3SAT $\in \mathcal{P}$, and hence that $\mathcal{P} = \mathcal{NP}$.

593.   ☜ The *knapsack problem* is defined as follows:

KNAPSACK

INSTANCE: Positive integers $s_1, s_2, \ldots, s_n, S$

QUESTION: Does there exist $X \subseteq \{1, 2, \ldots, n\}$ such that $\sum_{i \in X} s_i = S$?

It is known that KNAPSACK is $\mathcal{NP}$-complete. However, in Section 8.2 we saw a dynamic programming algorithm for the knapsack problem that runs in time $O(nS)$. Therefore, KNAPSACK $\in \mathcal{P}$, and hence $\mathcal{P} = \mathcal{NP}$.

594. ✏️✏️ 💡 ☺️𝒫 A *split Turing machine* is a variant of the Turing machine in which the input and the computation are each split into two parts. (To refresh your memory about standard Turing machines see, for example, Aho, Hopcroft, and Ullman [1].) The first part of the computation (which uses a Turing machine) has access to the first part of the input only, and the second part of the computation (which uses Boolean formula evaluation) has access both to the second part of the input and to the output of the first part of the computation. The first part of the input is a string of bits that is presented as input to a standard Turing machine in the usual manner, together with the representation, in unary, of a natural number k. The Turing machine computes in the normal manner, and produces an output of exactly k bits. The second part of the input is the encoding of a Boolean formula using the standard encoding scheme from Garey and Johnson [28].

A deterministic split Turing machine M is said to *accept* an input string $x\#y$, where $x \in \mathbf{B}^n$, $y \in \mathbf{B}^m$, iff y is the encoding of a Boolean formula F with k variables, and M on input $x\#1^k$ outputs a satisfying assignment for F. The *time* taken by a computation of a deterministic split Turing machine M on input $x\#y$ is the number of steps taken by M on input $x\#1^k$. The time complexity of M is defined to be

$$T_M(n,m) \quad = \quad \max\{t \mid \text{there is an } x\#y \text{ where } x \in \mathbf{B}^n, y \in \mathbf{B}^m, \text{ where } y \\ \text{encodes a Boolean formula on } k \text{ variables, such that the} \\ \text{computation of } M \text{ on input } x\#1^k \text{ takes time } t\}.$$

A nondeterministic split Turing machine M is said to *accept* an input string $x\#y$, where $x \in \mathbf{B}^n$, $y \in \mathbf{B}^m$, iff y is the encoding of a Boolean formula F with k variables, and some computation of M on input $x\#1^k$ outputs a satisfying assignment for F. The *time* taken by a computation of a deterministic split Turing machine M on input $x\#y$ is the minimum over all accepting computations of M of the number of steps taken by M on input $x\#1^k$. The time complexity of M is defined to be

$$T_M(n,m) \quad = \quad \max\{1\} \cup \{t \mid \text{there is an } x\#y \text{ where } x \in \mathbf{B}^n, y \in \mathbf{B}^m, \\ \text{where } y \text{ encodes a Boolean formula on } k \text{ variables, such} \\ \text{that } M \text{ takes time } t \text{ to accept } x\#1^k\}.$$

A split Turing machine M is said to run in *polynomial time* if there exists a polynomial p such that for all $m, n \geq 1$, $T_M(n,m) \leq p(n,m)$. The class split-$\mathcal{P}$ is then defined to be the set of languages accepted by a deterministic split Turing machine in polynomial time, and the class split-$\mathcal{NP}$ is defined to be the set of languages accepted by a nondeterministic split Turing machine in polynomial time.

We claim that split-$\mathcal{P} \neq$ split-$\mathcal{NP}$. The proof is as follows. Consider the language S that consists of the strings $\varepsilon\#y$ such that y is the encoding of a satisfiable Boolean formula F. Clearly, $S \in$ split-$\mathcal{NP}$, since the Turing machine on input $\varepsilon\#1^k$, where k is the number of variables in F, merely need guess an output string of k bits, which it can do in time linear in k, which is linear in the number of bits in y. However, S cannot be in split-$\mathcal{P}$, since the deterministic part of the computation has access only to the number of variables in F, and hence must give the same output for the two-variable Boolean formulae $x_1 \wedge x_2$ and $x_1 \wedge \overline{x}_2$. Both of these formulae are satisfiable, yet since there is no truth assignment that satisfies them both, any deterministic split Turing machine must make an error on one of them. Thus, $S \in$ split-$\mathcal{NP}$, and $S \notin$ split-$\mathcal{P}$, and so split-$\mathcal{P} \neq$ split-$\mathcal{NP}$.

Now, it is easy to see that $\mathcal{P} =$ split-$\mathcal{P}$. To see that $\mathcal{P} \subseteq$ split-$\mathcal{P}$, simply assume that $L \in \mathcal{P}$ is encoded in binary, and append to every member of L a fixed string encoding the identity formula. Clearly, this is a member of split-$\mathcal{P}$. To see that split-$\mathcal{P} \subseteq \mathcal{P}$, note that a deterministic Turing machine can simulate a split Turing machine with polynomial overhead in time by simply simulating the Turing machine part and then evaluating the Boolean formula on the result obtained. This implies that $\mathcal{P} =$ split-$\mathcal{P}$, and it can be similarly shown that $\mathcal{NP} =$ split-$\mathcal{NP}$. Hence, $\mathcal{P} =$ split-$\mathcal{P} \neq$ split-$\mathcal{NP} = \mathcal{NP}$.

12.4 Circuits

An *architecture* is a finite combinational circuit (that is, a circuit constructed without feedback loops) with the gate functions left unspecified. A *task* for an architecture is an input-output pair, and a *task set* is a finite set of tasks. The *loading problem* is the following: Given an architecture and a task set, find functions for each of the gates that enable the circuit to give the correct output for each corresponding input in the task set. The following questions deal with the decision problem version of the loading problem: Given an architecture and a task set, decide whether there exist functions for each of the gates that enable the circuit to give the correct output for each corresponding input in the task set. The problems in this section are from Parberry [63].

595. Show that the loading problem is $\mathcal{NP}$-complete.

596. Show that the loading problem for circuits of depth 2 is $\mathcal{NP}$-complete.

597. 🎓🎓 📖 Show that the loading problem for circuits of fan-in 3 is $\mathcal{NP}$-complete.

598. 🎓🎓🎓 📖 Show that the loading problem for circuits with node-function set consisting of disjunctions and conjunctions of literals is $\mathcal{NP}$-complete even for circuits with only four nodes.

A *cyclic circuit* is a network of gates that may have cycles. Time is quantized, and at each step, one or more of the gates reads its inputs, and computes a new output. All connections are directed, and self-loops are allowed. The gate-functions are limited to are conjunction, disjunction, and complement. The circuit is said to have *converged to a stable configuration* if the output of all gates remains fixed over time. Consider the following problems:

The Stable Configuration Problem (SNN)
INSTANCE: A cyclic circuit M.
QUESTION: Does M have a stable configuration?

599. 🎓🎓 📖 Show that SNN is $\mathcal{NP}$-complete.

600. 🎓🎓 📖 Show that SNN is $\mathcal{NP}$-complete for cyclic circuits of fan-in 2.

12.5   ONE-IN-THREE 3SAT

Consider the following variants of One-in-Three 3SAT:

One-in-Three 3SAT (O3SAT1)
INSTANCE: A list of clauses C in which each clause contains at most three literals.
QUESTION: Is there a truth assignment for C in which each clause contains exactly one true literal?

One-in-Three 3SAT (O3SAT2)
INSTANCE: A list of clauses C in which each clause contains exactly three literals.
QUESTION: Is there a truth assignment for C in which each clause contains exactly one true literal?

One-in-Three 3SAT (O3SAT3)
INSTANCE: A list of clauses C in which each clause contains exactly three variables, all uncomplemented.
QUESTION: Is there a truth assignment for C in which each clause contains exactly one true variable?

Balanced One-in-Three 3SAT (B3SAT)
INSTANCE: A list of clauses C in which each clause consists of three variables and every variable appears in exactly three clauses.
QUESTION: Is there a truth assignment for C in which each clause contains exactly one true variable?

O3SAT1 is the original version of the problem studied by Schaefer [68], and O3SAT3 is the version listed by Garey and Johnson [28]. In the following problems, you may assume that O3SAT1 is $\mathcal{NP}$-complete.

601. ☞ Prove that O3SAT2 is $\mathcal{NP}$-complete.

602. ☞ Prove that O3SAT3 is $\mathcal{NP}$-complete.

603. ☞☞ 🖎 Prove that B3SAT is $\mathcal{NP}$-complete.

12.6 FACTORIZATION

Let p_i denote the ith prime number, starting with $p_1 = 2$. The factorization problem is defined as follows:

FACTORIZATION
INSTANCE: A natural number, N.
OUTPUT: A list of pairs (p_i, a_i) for $1 \le i \le k$, such that $N = p_1^{a_1} p_2^{a_2} \cdots p_k^{a_k}$.

604. ☞ 💡 Prove that if $\mathcal{P} = \mathcal{NP}$, then FACTORIZATION can be solved in polynomial time.

The *Smarandache function*, $\eta: \mathbb{N} \to \mathbb{N}$, is defined as follows: $\eta(k)$ is the smallest $m \in \mathbb{N}$ such that k divides evenly into $m!$.

605. ☞☞ Prove that if FACTORIZATION can be solved in polynomial time, then the Smarandache function can be computed in polynomial time.

606. ☞☞ Prove that if the Smarandache function can be computed in polynomial time, then FACTORIZATION can be solved in polynomial time.

12.7 HINTS

594. A lot of the details of this proof are missing. Most of them are correct. At least one of them is wrong. It is up to you to discover which.

604. Prove a Turing reduction to the problem "is there a factor less than M."

12.8 SOLUTIONS

595–597. A solution to these problems can be found in Judd [41].

598. A solution to this problem can be found in Parberry [61].

599–600. A solution to this problem can be found in Parberry [63].

603. A solution to this problem can be found in Parberry [60]. However, the reduction is from O3SAT3, not O3SAT1 as requested; so technically you'll have to solve Problem 602 in order to complete this proof.

12.9 COMMENTS

578. Most textbooks (and classes) prove that if $A \leq_p^m B$ and $B \in \mathcal{P}$, then $A \in \mathcal{P}$, and omit the proof of this result saying only that it is "similar."

591. This problem came out of a conversation with B. Chitturi in 1994.

594. In a fever-induced dream in 1993 I hallucinated that I had succeeded in proving that $\mathcal{P} = \mathcal{NP}$, and this was the proof. I awoke at 3 A.M. and instantly knew that the proof was wrong (I was not *that* sick!).

595. For more information on the complexity of variants of the loading problem, consult also Judd [39, 40, 42], Lin and Vitter [53], and Blum and Rivest [12, 13].

Chapter 13

Miscellaneous

Here are some miscellaneous problems, defined to be those that do not necessarily fit into the earlier chapters, and those for which part of the problem is to determine the algorithmic technique to be used. You're on your own!

13.1 SORTING AND ORDER STATISTICS

This section contains questions on sorting and order statistics (the latter is a fancy name for "find the k smallest element"). These are mainly upper bounds. Problems on lower bounds are mostly (but not exclusively) found in Section 13.2.

607. 🎓 Show that n positive integers in the range 1 to k can be sorted in time $O(n \log k)$.

608. 🎓 Devise an algorithm for finding the k smallest elements of an unsorted set of n integers in time $O(n + k \log n)$.

609. 🎓🎓 Show that finding the median of a set S and finding the kth smallest element are reducible to each other. That is, if $|S| = n$, any algorithm for finding the median of S in time $T(n)$ can be used to design an $O(T(n))$ time algorithm for finding the kth smallest, and vice-versa, whenever the following holds: T is monotone increasing and there exists a constant $0 < c < 1$ such that $T(n/2) < c \cdot T(n)$ for $n \in \mathbb{N}$.

The *nuts and bolts* problem is defined as follows. You are given a collection of n bolts of different widths, and n corresponding nuts. You are allowed to try a nut and bolt together, from which you can determine whether the nut is too large, too small, or an exact match for the bolt, but there is no way to compare two nuts together, or two bolts together. You are to match each bolt to its nut.

610. 🎓🎓 ☺ Show that any algorithm for the nuts and bolts problem must take $\Omega(n \log n)$ comparisons in the worst case.

611. ☞☞ ☺☞ Devise an algorithm for the nuts and bolts problem that runs in time $O(n \log n)$ on average .

612. ☞ Suppose that instead of matching all of the nuts and bolts, you wish to find the smallest bolt and its corresponding nut. Show that this can be done with only $2n - 2$ comparisons.

13.2 LOWER BOUNDS

The lower bounds considered in this section are for what is known as *comparison-based* algorithms. These are algorithms that store their input in memory, and the only operations permitted on that data are comparisons and simple data movements (that is, the input data are not used for computing an address or an index). The two most common techniques used are the *adversary argument* and the *decision tree*.

613. ☞☞ Show a matching lower bound for the sorting problem of Problem 607 in a comparison-based model.

614. ☞ ☀ Prove that any comparison-based algorithm that searches a sorted array must make at least $\Omega(\log n)$ comparisons.

615. ☞ Show that any comparison-based algorithm for finding the median must use at least $n - 1$ comparisons.

616. ☞ Show that any comparison-based algorithm for finding the second-smallest of n values can be extended to find the smallest value also, without requiring any more comparisons to be performed.

617. ☞☞ Show that at least $n + \lfloor \log n \rfloor - 2$ comparisons are necessary to find the smallest and second smallest of a list of n items.

618. ☞ Show that any comparison-based algorithm for sorting can be modified to remove all duplicates without requiring any more comparisons to be performed.

619. ☞☞ Show that any comparison-based algorithm for removing duplicates from a list of values must use $\Omega(n \log n)$ comparisons.

620. ☞☞ Use decision trees to find a lower bound of

$$n + 0.5 \log n - 2.66$$

on the number of comparisons required to find the median. You may use Stirling's approximation,

$$n! \sim \sqrt{2\pi n}(n/e)^n.$$

621. ☞☞☞ Show that if each of the $n!$ permutations is equally likely, then the average key is about $n/3$ places from its proper position in sorted order. What does this say about the average case complexity of bubblesort?

13.3   GRAPH ALGORITHMS

This section contains general questions on graph algorithms. More graph algorithm problems can be found in Sections 2.10, 2.11, 7.7, 8.4, 9.2, 9.3, 9.4, and 13.4, and a few scattered in applications sections in various chapters.

622. ☞☞ An *ancestor query* for a tree is a request for information about the ancestor relationship between two nodes in the tree. It can be viewed as evaluating the function:

$$\text{ancestor}(v, w) = \begin{cases} -1 & \text{if } v \text{ is a proper ancestor of } w \\ 1 & \text{if } w \text{ is a proper ancestor of } v \\ 0 & \text{otherwise.} \end{cases}$$

Design and analyze an algorithm that takes a tree as input and preprocesses it so that ancestor queries can subsequently be answered in $O(1)$ time. Preprocessing of an n-node tree should take $O(n)$ time.

623. ☞☞ Let $G = (V, E)$ be a directed graph with n vertices. A *sink* is a vertex $s \in V$ such that for all $v \in V$, $(v, s) \notin E$. Devise an algorithm that, given the adjacency matrix of G, determines whether or not G has a sink in time $O(n)$.

624. ☞ Suppose a set of truck drivers work for a shipping company that delivers commodities between n cities. The truck drivers generally ignore their instructions and drive about at random. The probability that a given truck driver in city i will choose to drive to city j is p_{ij}. You may assume that for all $1 \leq i, j \leq n$, $0 \leq p_{ij} \leq 1$, and that for all $1 \leq i \leq n$, $\sum_{j=1}^{n} p_{ij} = 1$. Devise an algorithm that determines in time $O(n^3)$ the most probable path between cities i and j for all $1 \leq i, j \leq n$.

625. ☞☞ A graph is *triconnected* if there is no pair of vertices whose removal disconnects the graph. Design an algorithm that determines whether a graph with n vertices and e edges is triconnected in time $O(ne)$.

Let $G = (V, E)$ be a directed labeled graph with n vertices and e edges. Suppose the cost of edge (v, w) is $\ell(v, w)$. Suppose $c = (v_0, v_2 \ldots, v_{k-1})$ is a cycle, that is, $(v_i, v_{(i+1) \bmod k}) \in E$ for all $0 \leq i < k$. The *mean cost* of c is defined by

$$\mu(c) = \frac{1}{k} \sum_{i=0}^{k-1} w(v_i, v_{(i+1) \bmod k}).$$

Let μ be the cost of the minimum mean-cost cycle in G, that is, the minimum value of μ_c over all cycles c in G.

Assume without loss of generality that every $v \in V$ is reachable from a source vertex $s \in V$. Let $\delta(v)$ be the cost of the cheapest path from s to v, and $\delta_k(v)$ be the cost of the cheapest path of length exactly k from s to v (if there is no path from s to v of length exactly k, then $\delta_k(v) = \infty$).

626. ☞☞ Show that if $\mu = 0$, then G contains no negative-cost cycles and for all $v \in V$,

$$\delta(v) = \min_{0 \le k \le n-1} \delta_k(v).$$

627. ☞☞ ☀ Show that if $\mu = 0$, then for all vertices $v \in V$,

$$\max_{0 \le k \le n-1} \frac{\delta_n(v) - \delta_k(v)}{n - k} \ge 0.$$

628. ☞☞ ☀ Let c be a cycle of cost zero, and let u, v be any pair of vertices on c. Suppose that the cost of the path from u to v along c is x. Prove that $\delta(v) = \delta(u) + x$.

629. ☞☞ ☀ Show that if $\mu = 0$, then there exists a vertex v on the minimum mean-cost cycle such that

$$\max_{0 \le k \le n-1} \frac{\delta_n(v) - \delta_k(v)}{n - k} = 0.$$

630. ☞☞ Show that if $\mu = 0$, then

$$\min_{v \in V} \max_{0 \le k \le n-1} \frac{\delta_n(v) - \delta_k(v)}{n - k} = 0.$$

631. ☞☞ Show that if we add a constant c to the cost of every edge of G, then μ is increased by exactly c. Hence, show that

$$\mu = \min_{v \in V} \max_{0 \le k \le n-1} \frac{\delta_n(v) - \delta_k(v)}{n - k}.$$

632. ☞☞ Give an $O(ne)$ time algorithm to compute μ.

13.4 MAXIMUM FLOW

Suppose we are given a directed graph $G = (V, E)$ in which each edge $(u, v) \in E$ is labeled with a *capacity* $c(u, v) \in \mathbb{N}$. Let $s, t \in V$ be distinguished vertices called the *source* and *sink*, respectively. A *flow* in G is a function $f : E \to \mathbb{N}$ such that the following two properties hold:

- for all $e \in E$, $0 \le f(e) \le c(e)$, and
- for all $v \in V$, $v \ne s, t$,

$$\sum_{u \in V} f(u, v) = \sum_{u \in V} f(v, u)$$

(if $(u, v) \notin E$, we assume that $c(u, v) = f(u, v) = 0$).

The *total flow* of f is defined to be

$$\sum_{v \in V} f(v, s) - f(s, v).$$

The *maximum flow problem* is to find a flow f that has maximum total flow.

Algorithms for the maximum flow problem include the Ford-Fulkerson algorithm, the Dinic algorithm, and the Edmonds-Karp algorithm.

633. Let $G = (V, E)$ be a DAG. Devise and analyze an efficient algorithm to find the smallest number of directed vertex-disjoint paths that cover all vertices (that is, every vertex is on exactly one path).

634. Suppose we are given the maximum flow in a flow network $G = (V, E)$ with source s, sink t, and integer capacities. Suppose the capacity of a single edge is increased by one. Give an $O(n + e)$ algorithm for updating the maximum flow, where G has n vertices and e edges.

635. Suppose we are given the maximum flow in a flow network $G = (V, E)$ with source s, sink t, and integer capacities. Suppose the capacity of a single edge is decreased by one. Give an $O(n + e)$ algorithm for updating the maximum flow, where G has n vertices and e edges.

Consider a flow problem on a graph $G = (V, E)$ with n vertices and e edges with all capacities bounded above by a polynomial in n. For any given flow, let the *largest edge flow* be

$$\max_{(u,v) \in E} f(u, v).$$

636. Show that two different maximum flows in G can have different largest edge flows. Design an algorithm to find the minimum possible largest edge flow over all maximum flows in G in time $O(ne^2 \log n)$.

Suppose we are given the maximum flow in a flow network $G = (V, E)$ with source s, sink t, and integer capacities $c(u, v)$ on each edge $(u, v) \in E$. Suppose G has n vertices and e edges. The following modified version of the standard Ford-Fulkerson algorithm can be used to find a maximum flow in G.

> **function** max-flow-by-scaling(G, s, t)
> 1. $c := \max_{(u,v) \in E} c(u, v)$
> 2.   initialize flow f to zero
> 3. $k := 2^{\lceil \log c \rceil}$
> 4.   **while** $k \geq 1$ **do**
> 5.   **while** there exists an augmenting path p of capacity $\geq k$ **do**
> 6.   augment flow f along p
> 7. $k := k/2$
> 8.   **return**(f)

637. ☞☞ Prove that max-flow-by-scaling returns a maximum flow.

638. ☞☞ Show that the residual capacity of a minimum cut of G is at most $2ke$ whenever line 4 is executed.

639. ☞☞ Prove that the inner **while** loop of lines 5–6 is executed $O(e)$ times for each value of k.

640. ☞☞ Conclude from the statements of Problems 638–639 that max-flow-by-scaling can be implemented in time $O(e^2 \log c)$.

13.5 MATRIX REDUCTIONS

Consider two problems A and B that have time complexities $T_A(n)$ and $T_B(n)$, respectively. Problems A and B are said to be *equivalent* if $T_A(n) = \Theta(T_B(n))$. Some textbooks show that matrix multiplication is equivalent (under some extra conditions) to matrix inversion. Here are some more problems along this line:

641. ☞☞ ☀ ☞ Show that multiplying two $n \times n$ matrices is equivalent to squaring an $n \times n$ matrix.

642. ☞☞ ☀ Show that multiplying two $n \times n$ matrices is equivalent to cubing an $n \times n$ matrix.

643. ☞☞ ☀ Show that multiplying two $n \times n$ matrices is equivalent to raising an $n \times n$ matrix to the fourth power.

644. ☞☞ ☀ Show that for all $k \geq 2$, multiplying two $n \times n$ matrices is equivalent to raising an $n \times n$ matrix to the kth power.

645. 🎓 🎓 💡 Define the *closure* of an $n \times n$ matrix A to be $\sum_{i=0}^{\infty} A^i$, where A^0 is the $n \times n$ identity matrix, and for $k > 0$, $A^k = A \cdot A^{k-1}$, where "$\cdot$" denotes matrix multiplication. (Note that closure is not defined for all matrices.) Show that multiplying two $n \times n$ matrices is equivalent to computing the closure of an $n \times n$ matrix.

646. 🎓 🎓 Show that multiplying two $n \times n$ matrices is equivalent to multiplying two $n \times n$ lower triangular matrices.

647. 🎓 🎓 Show that multiplying two $n \times n$ matrices is equivalent to squaring an $n \times n$ lower triangular matrix.

648. 🎓 🎓 Show that multiplying two $n \times n$ matrices is equivalent to cubing an $n \times n$ lower triangular matrix.

649. 🎓 🎓 Show that multiplying two $n \times n$ matrices is equivalent to raising an $n \times n$ lower triangular matrix to the fourth power.

650. 🎓 🎓 Show that for all $k \geq 2$, multiplying two $n \times n$ matrices is equivalent to raising an $n \times n$ lower triangular matrix to the kth power.

651. 🎓 🎓 Show that multiplying $n \times n$ matrices is equivalent to computing the closure of an $n \times n$ lower triangular matrix. (See Problem 645 for the definition of matrix closure.)

13.6 GENERAL

652. 🎓 🎓 You are facing a high wall that stretches infinitely in both directions. There is a door in the wall, but you don't know how far away or in which direction. It is pitch dark, but you have a very dim lighted candle that will enable you to see the door when you are right next to it. Show that there is an algorithm that enables you to find the door by walking at most $O(n)$ steps, where n is the number of steps that you would have taken if you knew where the door is and walked directly to it. What is the constant multiple in the big-O bound for your algorithm?

653. 🎓 🎓 🎓 ☺ You are given an $n \times 2$ matrix of integers. You are allowed to permute the rows of the matrix as monolithic items, and to perform comparisons on the elements of the matrix. Your task is to find an $O(n \log n)$ time algorithm that permutes the rows so that neither column of the matrix contains an increasing subsequence (not necessarily contiguous) of length exceeding $\lceil \sqrt{n} \rceil$.

654. 🎓 🎓 It's Texas Chile Pepper day and you have a schedule of events that looks something like this:

$$
\begin{array}{lll}
8{:}30 & - & 9{:}15 \quad \text{Pepper Pancake Party} \\
9{:}30 & - & 10{:}05 \quad \text{Pepper Eating Contest} \\
9{:}50 & - & 11{:}20 \quad \text{Pepper Personality Profile} \\
9{:}00 & - & 11{:}00 \quad \text{Pepper Parade} \\
& \vdots &
\end{array}
$$

The schedule lists the times at which each event begins and ends. The events may overlap. Naturally, you want to attend as many events as you can. Design an efficient algorithm to find the largest set of nonoverlapping events. Prove that your algorithm is correct. How fast is it?

655. ☞☞ Let A be an $n \times n$ matrix of zeros and ones. A *submatrix* S of A is any group of contiguous entries that forms a square, more formally, $\{A[i,j] \mid \ell \le i \le \ell + k - 1, m \le j \le m + k - 1\}$ for some $1 \le \ell, m \le n$, $0 \le k \le \min(n - \ell + 1, n - m + 1)$. S is said to have *size* k. Design an algorithm that determines the size of the largest submatrix of ones in A in time $O(n^2)$.

656. ☞☞ We wish to compute the laziest way to dial an n-digit number on a standard push-button telephone using two fingers. We assume that the two fingers start out on the $*$ and $\#$ keys, and that the effort required to move a finger from one button to another is proportional to the Euclidean distance between them. Design and analyze an algorithm that computes in time $O(n)$ the method of dialing that involves moving your fingers the smallest amount of total distance.

657. ☞☞ Suppose $S = \{1, 2, \ldots, n\}$ and $f : S \to S$. If $R \subset S$, define $f(R) = \{f(x) \mid x \in R\}$. Devise an $O(n)$ time algorithm for determining the largest $R \subset S$ such that $f(R) = R$.

658. ☞☞ Let E be a set of m linear equations of the form $x_i = x_j + c_{ij}$ over the variables $x_1, \ldots, x_n$ ($c_{i,j} \in \mathbf{Z}$ for all $1 \le i, j \le n$). Devise an $O(m)$ time algorithm for determining whether the equations in E are consistent, that is, whether an assignment of integers can be made to the variables so that all of the equations in E are satisfied.

The following group of questions deals with the generalized version of the popular Sam Loyd 15-puzzle, called the $(n^2 - 1)$-puzzle. For definitions, see Problem 515.

659. ☞☞ 🎓 ☺♄ Design an algorithm for the $(n^2 - 1)$-puzzle that runs in time $O(n^3)$. Your algorithm must input a legal state of the puzzle and output a series of $O(n^3)$ moves that solves it.

660. ☞☞ 🎓 Show that the worst case number of moves needed to solve the $(n^2 - 1)$-puzzle is at least $n^3 - O(n^2)$.

661. ☜☞ 💡 Show that the average case number of moves needed to solve the $(n^2 - 1)$-puzzle is at least $2n^3/3 - O(n^2)$.

662. ☜☞ 💡 Show that for some constants $0 < \alpha, \beta < 1$, a random legal configuration of the $(n^2 - 1)$-puzzle requires at least αn^3 moves to solve with probability $1 - 1/e^{-\beta n^2}$.

Suppose you are given a collection of gold coins that includes a clever counterfeit (all the rest are genuine). The counterfeit coin is indistinguishable from the real coins in all measurable characteristics except weight. You have a scale with which you can compare the relative weight of coins. However, you do not know whether the counterfeit coin is heavier or lighter than the real thing. Your problem is to find the counterfeit coin and determine whether it is lighter or heavier than the rest.

663. ☜☞ 💡 📖 Show that if there are 12 coins, the counterfeit coin can be found in three weighings.

664. ☜☞ Show that if there are 39 coins, the counterfeit coin can be found in four weighings.

665. ☜☞ 💡 Show that if there are $n \geq 3$ coins, the counterfeit coin can be found in $\lceil \log_3 2n \rceil$ weighings.

666. ☜☞ Show that if there are $n \geq 3$ coins, at least $\lceil \log_3 2n \rceil$ weighings are needed to find the counterfeit coin.

Your job is to seat n rambunctious children in a theater with n balconies. You are given a list of m statements of the form "i hates j." If i hates j, then you do not want to seat i above or in the same balcony as j, otherwise i will throw popcorn at j instead of watching the play.

667. ☜☞ Give an algorithm that assigns the balconies (or says that it is not possible) in time $O(m + n)$.

668. ☜☞ Design and analyze an algorithm for finding the minimum number of balconies needed.

13.7   HINTS

614. Show that if the search for two different elements x, y, where $x < y$, in the set leads to the same leaf of the comparison tree, then the search for any element a of the universe with $x < a < y$ must also lead to that leaf, which contradicts the correctness of the algorithm.

627. Use both properties from Problem 626.

628. The cost of the path from v to u along c is $-x$.

629. Show that a min-cost path to any vertex on the minimum mean-cost cycle can be extended along the cycle to the next vertex on the cycle.

633. Suppose $V = \{v_1, \ldots, v_n\}$. Form a network $G' = (V', E')$ as follows.

$$
\begin{aligned}
V' &= \{s, t\} \cup \{x_1, \ldots, x_n\} \cup \{y_1, \ldots, y_n\}, \\
E' &= \{(s, x_i) \mid 1 \le i \le n\} \cup \{(y_i, t) \mid 1 \le i \le n\} \cup \{(x_i, y_i) \mid (v_i, v_j) \in E\}.
\end{aligned}
$$

The capacity of all edges is one. Show that the minimum number of paths that cover V in G is equal to $n - f$, where f is the maximum flow in G'.

636. Consider the Edmonds-Karp algorithm for maximum flow.

641–645. Consider Problems 647–651. The lower triangular property can actually make the problem easier, if you think about it for long enough. On the other hand, there do exist nontriangular solutions, as the solution to Problem 641 given later demonstrates.

659. Use a combination of greedy and divide-and-conquer techniques. Suppose the hole is immediately to the right of a square S. Let L, R, U, D denote moving the hole one place left, right, up, and down, respectively. Then the sequence of moves $ULDLUR$ moves S one square diagonally up and to the right. Use this sequence of moves, and others like it, to move each square to its correct space, stopping when there is not enough space left to perform the maneuver. Figure out how to finish it, and you've solved the problem! The best I can do is $5n^3 - \Omega(n^2)$ moves. Make sure that the configuration you come up with is solvable. It can be shown that if the hole is in the lower right corner, the solvable states of the puzzle are exactly those that can be made with an even number of transpositions.

660. The *Manhattan distance* of a tile in square (i, k) that belongs in square (k, ℓ) is defined to be $|i - k| + |j - \ell|$. The *Manhattan distance* of a configuration of the puzzle is defined to be the sum of the Manhattan distances of its tiles. Show that the Manhattan distance is a lower bound on the number of moves needed to solve the puzzle, and that there exists a configuration that has Manhattan distance at least $n^3 - O(n^2)$.

661. Find a lower bound for the average Manhattan distance.

662. Find a lower bound for the Manhattan distance of a random configuration. The best value that I can get for α is 16/243. You will need to use Chernoff bounds. Let $B(m, N, p)$ be the probability of obtaining at least m successes

out of N Bernoulli trials, each with probability p of success. The following result is a well-known consequence of the Chernoff bounds (see, for example, Angluin and Valiant [5] and Valiant and Brebner [80]): Let $\beta = m/Np - 1$. If $0 \leq \beta \leq 1$, then $\beta(m, N, p) \leq e^{-\beta^2 Np/2}$.

663. Start by dividing the coins into three piles of four coins. Pick two piles and compare their weights.

665. Start by solving Problems 663 and 664. Then generalize your solution.

13.8 SOLUTIONS

641. The trick is to embed A and B into a larger matrix that, when squared, has AB has a submatrix. The solution can then be read off easily in optimal (that is, $O(n^2)$) time. There are many embeddings that work, including

$$\begin{bmatrix} 0 & A \\ B & 0 \end{bmatrix}^2 = \begin{bmatrix} AB & 0 \\ 0 & AB \end{bmatrix}.$$

663. Actually, I'm not going to give you a solution. This problem is so popular with mathematicians that you ought to be able to find one in the literature somewhere. It even appears in a science fiction novel by Piers Anthony [6, Chapter 16].

13.9 COMMENTS

610. The nuts and bolts problem is from Rawlins [66].

611. This algorithm is mentioned in Alon et al. [4].

653. This problem was suggested to the author by Arny Rosenberg. Interestingly, one can prove by a counting argument that one can so permute an $n \times k$ matrix, but an actual efficient algorithm is known only for $k = 1, 2$. For $k = 1$, this is a relative of the Erdös-Szekeres Theorem , which states that there exists in every sequence of n integers a monotonic subsequence (either ascending or descending) of length $\lfloor \sqrt{n} \rfloor$ (for more recent proofs of this theorem, see, for example, Dijkstra [22], and Seidenberg [73]).

659. Horden [36] gives an interesting history of this puzzle and its variants. See also Gardner [27]. Early work on the 15-puzzle includes Johnson [38] and Storey [76]. The minimum number of moves to solve each legal permutation of the 8-puzzle has been found by exhaustive search by Schofield [69]. The minimum number of moves needed to solve the 15-puzzle in the worst case is unknown, but has been the subject of various papers in the AI literature,

including Michie, Fleming and Oldfield [57] and Korf [48]. Ratner and Warmuth [65] have proved that the problem of determining the minimum length number of moves for any given legal configuration of the $(n^2 - 1)$-puzzle is $\mathcal{NP}$-complete, and they demonstrate an approximation algorithm that makes no more than a (fairly large) constant factor number of moves than necessary for any given legal configuration. Kornhauser, Miller, and Spirakis [49] have shown an algorithm for the $(n^2 - 1)$-puzzle and its generalizations that always runs in time $O(n^3)$.

Bibliography

[1] A. V. Aho, J. E. Hopcroft, and J. D. Ullman. *The Design and Analysis of Computer Algorithms.* Addison-Wesley, 1974.

[2] A. V. Aho, J. E. Hopcroft, and J. D. Ullman. *Data Structures and Algorithms.* Addison-Wesley, 1983.

[3] A. V. Aho and J. D. Ullman. *Foundations of Computer Science.* Computer Science Press, 1992.

[4] N. Alon, M. Blum, A. Fiat, S. Kannan, M. Naor, and R. Ostrovsky. Matching nuts and bolts. In *Proc. 5th Annual Symposium on Discrete Algorithms*, pages 690–696, 1994.

[5] D. Angluin and L. Valiant. Fast probabilistic algorithms for Hamiltonian circuits and matchings. In *Proceedings of the Ninth Annual ACM Symposium on Theory of Computing*, pages 30–41. ACM Press, 1977.

[6] P. Anthony. *With a Tangled Skein*, volume 3 of *Incarnations of Immortality*. Ballantine Books, 1985.

[7] S. Baase. *Computer Algorithms: Introduction to Design and Analysis.* Addison-Wesley, 1978.

[8] W. W. Rouse Ball and H. S. M. Coxeter. *Mathematical Recreations and Essays.* University of Toronto Press, 12th edition, 1974.

[9] J. Bentley. *Programming Pearls.* Addison-Wesley, 1986.

[10] J. Bentley. *More Programming Pearls: Confessions of a Coder.* Addison-Wesley, 1988.

[11] B. Bernhardsson. Explicit solutions to the n-queens problem for all n. *SIGART Bulletin*, 2(2):7, 1991.

[12] A. Blum and R. L. Rivest. Training a 3-node neural network is NP-complete. In *Neural Information Processing Systems 1*, pages 494–501. Morgan Kaufmann, 1989.

[13] A. Blum and R. L. Rivest. Training a 3-node neural network is NP-complete. *Neural Networks*, 5(1):117–127, 1992.

[14] G. Brassard and P. Bratley. *Algorithmics: Theory and Practice*. Prentice Hall, 1988.

[15] A. Conrad, T. Hindrichs, H. Morsy, and I. Wegener. Wie es dem springer gelang, schachbretter beliebiger groesse und zwischen beliebig vorgegebenen anfangs- und endfeldern vollstaendig abzuschreiten. *Spektrum der Wissenschaft*, pages 10–14, February 1992.

[16] A. Conrad, T. Hindrichs, H. Morsy, and I. Wegener. Solution of the knight's Hamiltonian path problem on chessboards. *Discrete Applied Mathematics*, 50:125–134, 1994.

[17] S. A. Cook. The complexity of theorem proving procedures. In *Proceedings of the Third Annual ACM Symposium on Theory of Computing*, pages 151–158. ACM Press, 1971.

[18] D. Coppersmith and S. Winograd. Matrix multiplication via arithmetic progressions. *Journal of Symbolic Computation*, 9:251–280, 1990.

[19] T. H. Cormen, C. E. Leiserson, and R. L. Rivest. *Introduction to Algorithms*. MIT Press, 1990.

[20] P. Cull and J. DeCurtins. Knight's tour revisited. *Fibonacci Quarterly*, 16:276–285, 1978.

[21] E. W. Dijkstra. *A Discipline of Programming*. Prentice Hall, 1976.

[22] E. W. Dijkstra. Some beautiful arguments using mathematical induction. *Acta Informatica*, 13:1–8, 1980.

[23] P. Eades and B. McKay. An algorithm for generating subsets of fixed size with a strong minimal change property. *Information Processing Letters*, pages 131–133, 1984.

[24] L. Euler. Solution problematis ad geometriam situs pertinentis. *Comentarii Academiae Scientarum Petropolitanae*, 8:128–140, 1736.

[25] L. Euler. Solution d'une question curieuse qui ne paroit soumise à aucune analyse. *Mem. Acad. Sci. Berlin*, pages 310–337, 1759.

[26] S. Even. *Graph Algorithms*. Pitman, 1979.

[27] M. Gardner. *The Mathematical Puzzles of Sam Loyd.* Dover, 1959.

[28] M. R. Garey and D. S. Johnson. *Computers and Intractability: A Guide to the Theory of NP-Completeness.* W. H. Freeman, 1979.

[29] A. M. Gibbons. *Algorithmic Graph Theory.* Cambridge University Press, 1985.

[30] R. L. Graham, D. E. Knuth, and O. Patashnik. *Concrete Mathematics: A Foundation for Computer Science.* Addison-Wesley, 1989.

[31] R. L. Graham, B. L. Rothschild, and J. H. Spencer. *Ramsey Theory.* John Wiley & Sons, 1990.

[32] R. L. Graham and J. H. Spencer. Ramsey theory. *Scientific American,* 263(1), July 1990.

[33] D. H. Greene and D. E. Knuth. *Mathematics for the Analysis of Algorithms.* Birkhäuser, 1982.

[34] D. Harel. *Algorithmics: The Spirit of Computing.* Addison-Wesley, 1987.

[35] B. R. Heap. Permutations by interchanges. *Computer Journal,* 6:293–294, 1963.

[36] L. E. Horden. *Sliding Piece Puzzles.* Oxford University Press, 1986.

[37] E. Horowitz and S. Sahni. *Fundamentals of Computer Algorithms.* Computer Science Press, 1978.

[38] W. A. Johnson. Notes on the 15 puzzle 1. *American Journal of Mathematics,* 2(4):397–399, 1879.

[39] J. S. Judd. Learning in networks is hard. In *Proc. of the First International Conference on Neural Networks,* pages 685–692. IEEE Computer Society Press, 1987.

[40] J. S. Judd. *Neural Network Design and the Complexity of Learning.* PhD thesis, University of Massachusetts, Amherst, MA, 1988.

[41] J. S. Judd. On the complexity of loading shallow neural networks. *Journal of Complexity,* 4:177–192, 1988.

[42] J. S. Judd. *Neural Network Design and the Complexity of Learning.* MIT Press, 1990.

[43] R. M. Karp. Reducibility among combinatorial problems. In R. E. Miller and J. W. Thatcher, editors, *Complexity of Computer Computations.* Plenum Press, New York, 1972.

[44] J. H. Kingston. *Algorithms and Data Structures: Design, Correctness, Analysis*. Addison-Wesley, 1990.

[45] D. E. Knuth. *Fundamental Algorithms*, volume 1 of *The Art of Computer Programming*. Addison-Wesley, second edition, 1973.

[46] D. E. Knuth. *Sorting and Searching*, volume 3 of *The Art of Computer Programming*. Addison-Wesley, 1973.

[47] D. E. Knuth. *Seminumerical Algorithms*, volume 2 of *The Art of Computer Programming*. Addison-Wesley, second edition, 1981.

[48] R. E. Korf. Depth-first iterative deepening: An optimal admissible tree search. *Artificial Intelligence*, 27(1):97–109, 1985.

[49] D. Kornhauser, G. Miller, and P. Spirakis. Coordinating pebble motion on graphs, the diameter of permutation groups, and applications. In *25th Annual Symposium on Foundations of Computer Science*, pages 241–250. IEEE Computer Society Press, 1984.

[50] D. C. Kozen. *The Design and Analysis of Algorithms*. Springer-Verlag, 1992.

[51] C. W. H. Lam and L. H. Soicher. Three new combination algorithms with the minimal change property. *Communications of the ACM*, 25(8), 1982.

[52] Lewis and Denenberg. *Data Structures and Their Algorithms*. Harper Collins, 1991.

[53] J.-H. Lin and J. S. Vitter. Complexity results on learning by neural nets. *Machine Learning*, 6:211–230, 1991.

[54] X.-M. Lu. Towers of Hanoi problem with arbitrary $k \geq 3$ pegs. *International Journal of Computer Mathematics*, 24:39–54, 1988.

[55] E. Lucas. *Récréations Mathématiques*, volume 3. Gauthier-Villars, 1893.

[56] U. Manber. *Introduction to Algorithms: A Creative Approach*. Addison-Wesley, 1989.

[57] D. Michie, J. G. Fleming, and J. V. Oldfield. A comparison of heuristic, interactive, and unaided methods of solving a shortest-route problem. In D. Michie, editor, *Machine Intelligence 3*, pages 245–255. American Elsevier, 1968.

[58] B. M. E. Moret and H. D. Shapiro. *Design and Efficiency*, volume 1 of *Algorithms from P to NP*. Benjamin/Cummings, 1991.

[59] C. H. Papadimitriou and K. Steiglitz. *Combinatorial Optimization: Algorithms and Complexity*. Prentice Hall, 1982.

[60] I. Parberry. On the computational complexity of optimal sorting network verification. In *Proceedings of The Conference on Parallel Architectures and Languages Europe,* in Series *Lecture Notes in Computer Science,* volume 506, pages 252–269. Springer-Verlag, 1991.

[61] I. Parberry. On the complexity of learning with a small number of nodes. In *Proc. 1992 International Joint Conference on Neural Networks,* volume 3, pages 893–898, 1992.

[62] I. Parberry. Algorithms for touring knights. Technical Report CRPDC-94-7, Center for Research in Parallel and Distributed Computing, Dept. of Computer Sciences, University of North Texas, May 1994.

[63] I. Parberry. *Circuit Complexity and Neural Networks.* MIT Press, 1994.

[64] P. W. Purdom Jr. and C. A. Brown. *The Analysis of Algorithms.* Holt, Rinehart, and Winston, 1985.

[65] D. Ratner and M. K. Warmuth. The $(n^2 - 1)$-puzzle and related relocation problems. *Journal for Symbolic Computation,* 10:11–137, 1990.

[66] G. Rawlins. *Compared to What? An Introduction to the Analysis of Algorithms.* Computer Science Press, 1991.

[67] G. J. Rawlins. *Compared to What?: An Introduction to the Analysis of Algorithms.* Computer Science Press, 1992.

[68] T. J. Schaefer. The complexity of satisfiability problems. In *Proceedings of the Tenth Annual ACM Symposium on Theory of Computing,* pages 216–226. ACM Press, 1978.

[69] P. D. A. Schofield. Complete solution of the eight puzzle. In N. L. Collins and D. Michie, editors, *Machine Intelligence 1,* pages 125–133. American Elsevier, 1967.

[70] A. Schönhage and V. Strassen. Schnelle multiplikation grosser zahlen. *Computing,* 7:281–292, 1971.

[71] A. J. Schwenk. Which rectangular chessboards have a knight's tour? *Mathematics Magazine,* 64(5):325–332, 1991.

[72] R. Sedgewick. *Algorithms.* Addison-Wesley, 1983.

[73] A. Seidenberg. A simple proof of a theorem of Erdös and Szekeres. *Journal of the London Mathematical Society,* 34, 1959.

[74] J. D. Smith. *Design and Analysis of Algorithms.* PWS-Kent, 1989.

[75] D. Solow. *How to Read and Do Proofs.* Wiley, second edition edition, 1990.

[76] W. E. Storey. Notes on the 15 puzzle 2. *American Journal of Mathematics*, 2(4):399–404, 1879.

[77] R. Susic and J. Gu. A polynomial time algorithm for the n-queens problem. *SIGART Bulletin*, 1(3):7–11, 1990.

[78] Y. Takefuji. *Neural Network Parallel Computing*. Kluwer Academic Publishers, 1992.

[79] Y. Takefuji and K. C. Lee. Neural network computing for knight's tour problems. *Neurocomputing*, 4(5):249–254, 1992.

[80] L. G. Valiant and G. J. Brebner. A scheme for fast parallel communication. *SIAM Journal on Computing*, 11(2):350–361, 1982.

[81] J. Veerasamy and I. Page. On the towers of Hanoi problem with multiple spare pegs. *International Journal of Computer Mathematics*, 52:17–22, 1994.

[82] M. A. Weiss. *Data Structures and Algorithm Analysis*. Benjamin/Cummings, 1992.

[83] H. S. Wilf. *Algorithms and Complexity*. Prentice Hall, 1986.

Index

truth assignment, 148, 149, 152–154
Turing machine, 151

union-find, 135, 142, 145

vertex cover, 110

warehouse, 94, 95, 98
weighing matrix, 128
weighted median, 80

zero-one knapsack problem, 89